Praise for *The Gift of Restlessness: A Spirituality for Unsettled Seasons*

"This elegantly written book is, to use Parker Palmer's phrase, 'a paradoxical pearl of great price.' As the author writes about 'the little graces hidden' in the seasons of our lives, I found myself encountering hidden graces on nearly every page. This book is honest and raw and real, unafraid to wade into the waters of restlessness, to help us understand that it is not a pain to be avoided but a gift to be received. And because the writer was unafraid, I felt myself becoming less afraid and more welcoming of something I once feared, but now see as an ally in my formation."

—James Bryan Smith, author of
The Good and Beautiful God

"More nights than not, I awake at 3:30 a.m. with my heart racing and my mind fluttering. I don't sleep much. I wonder during those early mornings if there is something terribly wrong with me. I'm a restless one. For the last few years, I've seen those restless nights, the tossing and turning, as a problem to be fixed. But in *The Gift of Restlessness*, Casey Tygrett has me wondering. What if those restless nights are an invitation of the soul, an opportunity for me to ask the harder, deeper questions about my relationship with God? Perhaps you, too, need a reset for the restlessness of your soul; a new way of noting and noticing what God is up to in your life. If so, *The Gift of Restlessness* is the balm you've been looking for, and Casey is just the right guide."

—**Sean Palmer**, pastor, speaker, and author
of *Speaking by the Numbers, Unarmed Empire,*
and *Forty Days on Being a Three*

"I love it when a book challenges me to do a hard double-take: to look again at familiar territory in my life and see it with fresh eyes. Casey Tygrett's wonderful book does exactly this. How can restlessness serve as a 'skilled leader' for my spiritual journey? What can I learn from the Lord's Prayer if I approach it as a 'prayer of the restless nomad'? Tygrett delves into these transformative questions with honesty, rigor, and grace. Drawing on both his own life experience and the richness of Scripture, Tygrett reimagines each line of the Lord's Prayer as a holy container, revealing the surprising ways in which restlessness, unsettledness, and even irritation can open us up to deep and lasting spiritual maturity. Rather than resisting restlessness, or judging it as unholy, Tygrett invites us to *listen* to our dissatisfactions with curiosity, patience, and wonder. *The Gift of Restlessness* is a much-needed gift for the contemporary church, and I am grateful to have it!"

—**Debie Thomas**, columnist for *The Christian Century*
and author of *Into the Mess and Other Jesus Stories*

"What Casey Tygrett does with this book provides language for a vital and deeply human aspect of spiritual practice. *The Gift of Restlessness* sets readers free to be fully human in our pursuit of God, rather than feel like we have to transcend our humanity in order to be spiritual."

—**Justin McRoberts**, author of *Sacred Strides*

"Are seasons of wilderness and restlessness gifts or curses? Are they something to be avoided, overcome, or embraced as a path toward authentic growth and wholeness? In *The Gift of Restlessness*, Casey Tygrett turns the standard answer I've encountered in Christian teaching on its head and suggests—no, demonstrates, through his own life—that restlessness is not only a common and persistent spiritual state but it's also a *gift*. Tygrett meets us at the trailheads of six common restless-adjacent questions arising in our lives and walks with us as we live in a now-and-not-yet state with hope, joy, and curiosity. I can think of no better guide to join on that journey."

—**Jeff Crosby**, author of *The Language of the Soul*

"In *The Gift of Restlessness*, Casey Tygrett comes alongside us as a refreshing, non-anxious presence, a companion amid a tension-filled journey. Tygrett offers us wisdom and comfort out of a deep well. He shows us how it is possible to live, and even flourish, 'between wild beasts and angels.' I, for one, need wise ones like Tygrett to help anchor me in a world full of cacophonous voices inside and outside of the church—voices that lead me away from the good, true, and beautiful and toward the counterfeit. This is a beautiful book, born of hard-won insight."

—**Marlena Graves**, author of *The Way Up Is Down* and *Forty Days on Being a Nine*

"Like a contemporary Augustine, Casey Tygrett confesses his way through restlessness in his spiritual life and physical life. He makes us feel a little less alone in our moments of desperation or boredom, or even the absence of both. He asks us to pay attention to the absence of what we want or the absence of what we think we need, and to trust that in that liminal space, God is there still."

—**Lore Ferguson Wilbert**, author of
A Curious Faith and *Handle with Care*

THE GIFT OF RESTLESSNESS

CASEY TYGRETT

THE GIFT OF RESTLESSNESS

A SPIRITUALITY FOR UNSETTLED SEASONS

Broadleaf Books
Minneapolis

THE GIFT OF RESTLESSNESS
A Spirituality for Unsettled Seasons

The author is represented by the literary agent Don Gates @ The Gates Group, www.the-gates-group.com.

Cover image: Background: shutterstock/AVN Photo Lab; branch: shutterstock/Vera NewSib
Cover design: Gearbox Studio

Print ISBN: 978-1-5064-8356-6
eBook ISBN: 978-1-5064-8357-3

To Holley and Bailey for loving and living out all the gifts restlessness has given us.
And to BBD for being an endless source of stories and joy.

CONTENTS

INTRODUCTION

Frost sparkles underfoot as Winston and I make our sun-less trot into the backyard. It is 2:30 a.m., and the night is as quiet as an infant in deep sleep. I put him on a leash because we don't yet have a fence. I pull on my coat and slip my bare feet into my well-beaten boots. And we walk wandering circles around the yard.

Then I wait for Winston. Being that he has miniature innards, this bathroom trip takes place every four hours or so. Weather doesn't matter, nor does the weight of sleep on my eyelids. Like an old ad for the postal service, in rain, sleet, snow, or hail, we are there.

This moment can't be rushed, mainly because Winston isn't in a hurry. He has nowhere else he needs to be. Pensive and purposeful in sniffing every breeze floating by, he is present to the moment in front of him. The immediate is enough. He needs nothing more than this.

My wife will tell you that Winston and I often stand side by side in the yard and stare off into the green space behind the house. We apparently cock our heads the same way, creating the illusion of man and dog united in thought and intention. We aren't.

Winston lives contented with the seconds as they tick by, but my longing is for the warmth of my bed and the comfort of a few more hours of sleep. Yet even though I long to return to bed, I also resist the dawn of a new day. Even in these predawn hours, my mind is turning over the various details of life: work, relationships, questions, and struggles. Winston gently points his nose toward a new scent: *Rabbit? Coyote?* He lifts one paw and turns his snout to the air. Nothing else matters to him but that very question.

When Winston the Westie came into our lives in September 2020, I used those nightly walks to ponder when that season of life would end. We were living through the aching present tense of a global pandemic, wondering when some semblance of normalcy would burst through the door again. The coronavirus pandemic brought many of us to a restless moment. We knew we could never go back to life as it was. We could not stay in the shutdown forever without significant financial and spiritual consequences. Nor could we go back to the blissful naivete of prepandemic life.

The middle-of-the-night, aching, present-tense questions were—and remain—numerous. Likely you have your own. Perhaps your faith has changed and you've moved on to new expressions of life with God. You gave away the books that once inspired you and unsubscribed from *that* podcast. But what now? What community and content will shape you now?

Or perhaps we carry a memory, a scene in our minds. In that scene our former spouse and their new spouse share a tender look over the gift table at our son's graduation party. We think, *Is this how it will always be?* Or we go to another friend's wedding with no relationship or plans of our own. We begin to wonder if the phrase "always a bridesmaid, never a bride" was created specifically for us.

Winston sniffs and paws at the ground and finds a few rabbit droppings to munch on. I used to protest, but at some point, when it comes to creatures who have the evolutionary pedigree to hunt small game, you must pick your battles. For Winston, the darkness is filled with good things: little gifts spread around, which go unnoticed unless a snout and paws explore the lowest spots in the yard.

Winston sees the night as filled with opportunity, and he greets the unknown with delight. But I don't. Exhausted, worn to the bone, and even somewhat depressed, I watch Winston, who now sits on the diamond-sparkle grass as if he senses my energy level dipping. The dog is content to remain in the darkened present tense. For me, the end of the present moment can't come fast enough.

No one asks for restless moments: those times of feeling irritated, unsettled. No one. I don't ask to be outside with a dog at two-thirty in the morning, mounting fervent prayers for quick urination. We don't ask for faith crises, nor do we petition those we love to wound us or leave us. We don't usually ask for growth—spiritual, personal, emotional—but growth comes. And though growth is good and hopeful, it also comes with a measure of pain and uncertainty. We long to be anywhere but here, in this particular *nowness*. And yet, as philosopher

Dallas Willard says, "No one yet has found a way to live outside of the present moment." So here we are.

On that night in 2020, in the quiet, frosted land with an unhurried dog, I reckon with my restlessness—and not only the restlessness but also the accompanying fear, anxiety, and confusion that spring up when we are in that strange land in between dark and dawn.

Winston turns. It is time to go in. I lead him to the porch, where my wife, Holley, waits. She tenderly wipes his paws and unclasps the collar. Soon I will pick him up and dig my fingertips into his scruff, whispering and shushing and carrying him through the house.

I turn to lock the door and look one more time at the quiet void. Just like the night before. Just like the night yet to come. There are so many questions out there in the soft and soundless darkness. So much unknown. And yet there is so much of Spirit as well. It seems that both holy and haunting things live in those spaces we'd rather avoid.

So is there any point to this restlessness? Can there be goodness in the dark? Can we find little graces hidden in these midnight seasons of our lives? Is it possible that the unasked-for, unwanted, unbidden moments are thick with the Divine?

WHAT IS RESTLESSNESS?

For the sake of a definition, let's say that restlessness is the state of being irritated or unsettled by the present-tense realities of our lives. In that state we feel confined to the present moment, unable to go back to the way things were before but unsure about what lies ahead.

I have a strange kinship with restlessness. The restless moment in the cold dark with Winston when he was a puppy was far from my first. It followed a series of irritated, restless moments, perhaps even a lifetime of them.

Every six months or so, I enter the unsettled present tense. Maybe you do too. Like a kind old soul, restlessness sidles up to us and claps us on the shoulder, waving a gnarled hand over our life and whispering, "All of this needs to change." We can call it boredom, dissatisfaction, or feeling stuck—restlessness nods in agreement with each description.

So I try to grow a beard or change my social media profile picture. I change up morning routines or my email tagline. I go looking to see what new jobs are out in the wider world.

Likely you have your methods for engaging your own restlessness. We take a dopamine hit by clicking "Buy Now." Perhaps listening to a new podcast lightens the heavy load of your irritation. As a pastor, I know dear folks who encountered restlessness by changing religious communities for reasons as simple as "it was time to move on." In some cases, we change our partner or our job to try to dismantle our unsettled state.

No matter what coping mechanism we choose, an encounter with restlessness is unavoidable. In fact, I believe restlessness is one of the most common and consistent spiritual states in life. Though our particulars are different, the overall experience is the same. We look up and recognize the land in between. Whatever the cause and consequences, in these seasons, the strong feeling speaks clearly: Things need to change—but what, how, and why?

In the journey of spiritual transformation, this is especially true. We share in the greater drama of the Divine's unfolding mercy, though our lines and stage directions differ. Our steps of transformation follow our own unique personality, situation, and history. Yet we also overlap with each other. In the things of "me," there is always resonance with the greater "we." And in this spiritual journey, regardless of our hesitation or denial, restlessness is part of the shaping of our souls. All of us. Restlessness is a group project.

Though these unsettled states are cast as negative, that isn't always the case. Sometimes restlessness is rooted in hopeful anticipation. When we approach the end of high school or college or graduate school, the restlessness includes the relief of the burden of school and excitement about the new opportunities to work our way into the world. When we come close to completing a creative project, hungry to see the ripples God creates in the wider world, we feel restless too. As a baby's arrival date inches closer or the hard work of the adoption process ends, a beautiful and mysterious story of longing is written within us, and it may feel a lot like restlessness.

Restlessness often describes longing, hope, and desire in ways that words and images cannot. As the late Irish poet and philosopher John O'Donohue says, "Desire is often expressed in restlessness."

Yet there are more troubling forms of restlessness, and these are the forms that occupy our attention. A relationship ends in fire and anger, our empty nest reveals surprising cracks in our marriage, our child's decision fills us with anxiety about their future, or a global pandemic reveals political divisions we hadn't noticed before.

In all the restless spaces we encounter, the language of bartenders at closing time comes to mind: "You don't have to go home, but you can't stay here." Or perhaps more accurately: "You *can't* go home, but you can't stay here." We have left the familiar for the wider unknown life. We cannot go back to the way things used to be—in our relationships, or our work, or our faith—but the way forward is not yet clear.

So here we are.

CAN'T GO HOME, CAN'T STAY HERE

"It seems that we are born with a memory in our hearts of where we've been and consciousness of where we're going," writer Joan Chittister remarks. "Nothing else satisfies along the way." I agree, mostly. In many of my restless seasons however, I haven't had that clear consciousness of where I am headed. The way ahead appeared, but it was gray and clouded. At that point, the restlessness that unsettles us at the core presses us firmly into our present-tense realities. We cannot move—we feel paralyzed.

"My God, my God, why have you forsaken me?" David cries out in Psalm 22:1. Buried in this phrase is both the memory of an unforsaken life and the anguish of not knowing what this new forsakenness means. David is crying from the place between a life once unforsaken and the place where the Divine returns to him again. He is cemented in the restless present tense. The cry rises from a sweet memory of being cared for, and now, in the absence of that, the way forward is clouded and obscure.

The moment in front of him—or in our case, the suffering, the loneliness, the lost feeling of joblessness or fading health—is the focus of forsakenness. Even Jesus expresses this longing, this desperation, as he quotes David's cry while in the present-tense suffering of a Roman cross.

When we are in the throes of restlessness, our cries to the Divine are built primarily on a fixed space within the present—the hard edges of life right before our eyes. We cannot go back to the time before we heard "I'm not sure this marriage is going to work out" or "I'm sorry; she didn't make it." But we also have no idea what comes next.

And so we stand in line at the grocery store, our feet like concrete pilings driven through the cheap linoleum. We don't see others around us, and we can't focus on the tabloids or thirty-five brands of wintergreen mints. The bartender's message, amended a bit, keeps running through our minds: you can't go home, but you can't stay here.

In those restless moments, where do we go? What do we do?

CHAPTER 1

BETWEEN THE BEASTS AND THE ANGELS

The clipboard wobbles in my hand. Sitting on well-worn furniture, stained by years of people sipping (and spilling) stale coffee, I wait, just as they waited.

Perhaps they waited for answers. They waited for their turn to talk to a professional and to get a diagnosis. Listening for their name, they looked through the floor-to-ceiling windows into an open courtyard—the same windows I look through now, assessing the deepening darkness outside. Waiting rooms like this one are strange places of in-betweenness.

There is no liturgy, no scripted prayer, no holy language that provides full relief when a loved one is in physical or emotional distress. My wife and I are here with our daughter, who is having a mental health crisis. We are checking her into an inpatient behavioral health center.

No one is prepared for their child to suffer. We didn't plan for this when we painted her nursery. When we dropped her off for the first day of first grade and believed, naively, that that moment was the height of sadness. We couldn't have imagined. Yet here I am, unsteady. Restless. I can't go back to those kinder days, but I can't stay in this lobby either.

Holley has gone in with my daughter, as pandemic restrictions only allow for one parent with their child in the treatment areas. The lobby is now quiet, save for the sound of staff entering and leaving. The shifts are changing. The kind woman behind the desk informs me that the lobby will close in thirty minutes and that after that I'll have to wait in my car. I nod. I can smell the hand sanitizer on my hands even through my mask. In the corner of the lobby, the TV runs one of those property rehab shows. Someone is getting a subway tile backsplash in their kitchen. "We've run into problems with the electrical system," the contractor says with a sigh. Drama.

It's August. School is starting soon. What will my daughter do then? Do we need to contact someone at the school?

The couple on TV chooses to put on a new porch. They need the outdoor space for all the entertaining they want to do. We haven't seen people in so long, I think. The pandemic presses in as I think about our empty entertaining spaces.

And then come the questions, unsurprisingly. Did we fail as parents? Did we miss a sign that she was in trouble? In this swelling storm of questions, I can't fix my gaze on any one point. I lean back and close my eyes. I play a game on my phone and then pray a bit, though the words won't come. Spirit is here, I know. But I want to be *anywhere* else but here.

"Sir, we're closing the lobby. You'll have to wait outside." I nod to the receptionist and hand her the clipboard. I gather my things and give one last look at the property rehab drama. Everyone seems very excited. Ceramic tile flooring has just gone into the new bathroom! The credits begin to roll. In that filtered world, scripted and edited for time, no real questions are asked or answered. I suppose that's why we love those fantasy worlds: we meet people who are so disengaged from our own restlessness that we can join them outside the fray.

In other spaces, people just like me are facing their own unsettled questions. Fingering a stack of bills, wondering, "Do I have enough to survive?" Glancing up from outdated magazines in a doctor's office, waiting to see if they could be well again. Could they be healed?

"Everything that happens to us has the potential to deepen us," John O'Donohue remarks. While that sounds lovely, I wonder, as I leave the lobby, if "everything" includes *this*. What gift could Spirit possibly give in the pitch of this sunless evening?

In the dark that deepens, we are forced to ask the questions that draw us deeper and deeper into the life of Spirit, the life of the Divine. We understand dependence on the Divine more and more as we release our need to see our way out of our restless present tense. But we must be led to those questions—and it turns out that restlessness is a skilled leader.

Restlessness leads us into fundamentally human questions—questions about belonging, purpose, provision, healing, and protection. When we ask them boldly, they reveal a gift within the restlessness. The gift is a flinty, formidable spirituality that moves us into and through our restless seasons.

WHAT WE DO IN THE WILD PLACES

The wilderness is a helpful metaphor for our spiritual journey, especially in restless seasons. It is a restless place: an irritated, unsettled space where all the common markers of place and person and safety are removed. Our false self—the "us" we pretend is true—cannot survive in the wilderness because desolation has no tolerance for pretense. In the imagery of the Bible, wilderness is where the hardest work of life with God is done. Wilderness places, also called "desolate" places in scripture, become divine places in mere moments.

The wilderness is where we meet the Divine because it dismantles our dependency on anything *other* than the Divine.

In Exodus, Moses goes to the wilderness because he is no longer welcomed among the Egyptians who raised him and because the Hebrews who share his DNA think he wants more power than he deserves. Wilderness is the restless space where he feels no attachment—only isolation. He doesn't choose to go there, but he goes anyway. "Who am I now?" Moses wonders as he wanders in the desolate places.

The Divine then sets the desolation on fire for a single purpose: to say, "I know you. I AM eternality, beauty, grace, and gravity, and I *know* you." Gone are both the comfortable status of being an Egyptian prince and the weight of his murderous rage. Moses's formation deepens and expands because he is willing to turn aside and face the restless blaze in that wilderness.

In an unsettled season, even there, Moses is *known*. In our own restlessness, we are fully known as well.

The wilderness may be a gift to Moses; it is an unsettled place, but it is also a deepening place with the Divine. Yet as quickly as it fills with sacredness, the wilderness begins the work of stripping people down. A fire burns away the crisis and the chaos. Tearing away all the artificial and the assumed, the comfortable and the customary, restlessness exposes reality as it is. If there is anything that matters in our restless journey of transformation, it is that we grasp *reality*. Transformation always begins with a realistic interrogation of what *is*.

Many people have written about faith deconstruction, the process of disillusionment some who have been raised in churches undergo. And much of the critique levied against those who are in the process of deconstructing their faith is that they're just trying to be in vogue—that they've been swayed to join the crowd. That may be true from time to time. But deconstruction is the search for what is real about faith, what is generative, what gives hope, and what draws us out of the darkness and into the light. Then when the light returns, we build something new, vibrant, and generative. This new construction is often stronger as well. This wilderness of tearing down and building up calls us to wander and discover. We follow that call because we know Spirit is there, but we have no idea what that means. We also know we cannot go back to faith as usual.

"Dissatisfaction becomes the spiritual director of our souls," Joan Chittister writes. "Without the dissatisfaction of the soul, how would we ever find our way to more?"

A WAY THROUGH

Many years after Moses, Jesus points the way to the wilderness once again. As the prophet calling with the voice of holy dissatisfaction, Jesus begins his journey with an unsettling act. At the beginning of his public life, Jesus joins John the Baptist in the water in a distinct act of repentance and forgiveness.

Jesus unsettles a whole world of belief in the Jordan River, but he isn't grandstanding or attempting to create a stir. When we submerge ourselves in the restless moments, we aren't looking to create some name for ourselves. In truth, we don't have much of a choice. Our unsettled, irritated stirrings simply send us searching.

The first message from the Divine to Jesus after the baptism ruckus is this: "You are my beloved, in whom I am well pleased." This belovedness sounds like the opposite of restlessness in so many ways. I believe that belovedness is the anchoring principle of the spiritual journey. Without belovedness, our restlessness will consume us.

Yet belovedness does not fix our unsettled, irritated states. Instead, it gives us a way through.

The crux of our problem with restlessness is that we think it's a sign of regression or spiritual immaturity. We don't see it as a gift. We believe that the outcome of spiritual formation—the process of becoming like Jesus in the skin we're in—is to be *immune* to restlessness. When we truly follow Spirit, we think, we experience constant calm and peace and rest.

But the careful journey of spiritual formation *inspires* restlessness rather than inoculating us against it. Restlessness isn't an obstacle to a set of deeply human gifts; it is a *signpost* we find in everyday things. "Our hearts are restless until they find rest in you," St. Augustine famously prayed. Spiritual formation draws restlessness in its wake.

So what if we would take a different posture with the Divine when it comes to restlessness? What if we see restlessness as a guiding gift—the generous permission to allow what irritates and unsettles us to move us closer and closer to who God is and, ultimately, who we are?

UNWILLING BUT GOING ANYWAY

Restlessness presses us into our neurological response cycle known as the limbic system, or the "lizard brain." It is the part of our brain that responds to restlessness via one of three responses I call *fight, flee,* or *flop.* I have noticed these responses in my own experiences with restlessness over the years. When that kind old soul that is restlessness remarks, "All of this must change," my brain responds in one of three ways.

Sometimes I *fight* against the feeling that something must change by forcing myself to believe this restless moment isn't important or helpful. I'll just read something new, watch a TED Talk, or switch up a routine, and everything will be fine again. The soul loves a good "muscle up" moment at first, but it fails to fully satisfy. Choosing to *flee* via distractions—such as food, technology, or alcohol—also comes to mind. When there is no end in sight, we sometimes try to forget the discussion even exists. Desperation is the final stop—the *flop* that means giving up. Succumbing to restlessness, I am tempted to say, "This will never change, and the only choice I have is to let it take me down." Despair becomes a far more welcome companion than whatever lies on the other side of the irritation and instability. All three of these responses share a common belief: the assumption that the questions inherent in restlessness must be eliminated.

Here I must be completely transparent: after years of study, conversation, and prayer, I haven't found a way *out* of restlessness. I'm convinced such a way doesn't exist.

If you are not convinced that restlessness is part of the transformational journey, notice that belovedness leads Jesus not to bliss but to the wilderness. Immediately after the baptism, Jesus goes to the deserted, wild places—just like Moses did, just like the nation of Israel did, and just like John the Baptist did. "Jesus was led up by the Spirit to the wilderness to be tempted."

Perhaps Jesus didn't even want to go to the wilderness; perhaps he had to be "led." But wilderness was where Spirit was headed. So, desirous of the desolate or not, Jesus followed. Spirit's way, it appears, is a way *into* and *through* unsettled seasons rather than a way *out*.

In the wilderness, then, the accuser (aka Satan) draws these limbic responses to the surface with three very human temptations. The temptations draw on a singular challenge that we find in our own restless moments: Are you really who you think you are or who the Divine says you are? Are you *really* God's beloved? Without belovedness, the compass is broken and we lose our grounding.

Henri J. M. Nouwen categorizes Jesus's three temptations in terms that we understand from our own wrestling matches with restlessness. He names them as the temptations to be relevant, to be powerful, and to be spectacular. These are the broader categories for the very human questions that call to us daily: questions of belonging and purpose, questions of contentment and healing, and questions of protection and rescue.

Belovedness always exists in tension with relevance, power, and spectacle. Can we manage the spectacular task of raising our kids while keeping our sanity? Can we power up and get our various responsibilities done—and with a relaxed smile on our face? Will our depression and anxiety destroy us in the end? Or should we just pretend that it really isn't as bad as it seems? How do we mend the political—which are also the personal—divides in our families? Or should we just stop giving our opinion and go into stealth mode?

Into these questions and others enter the typical responses: fight, flee, or flop. Yet Jesus's response is quite different. Jesus engages each temptation with wisdom and grace. He does not fight, and he certainly doesn't flee. Giving in isn't even a possibility.

REMAINING WITH A PURPOSE

Instead of fighting or fleeing or even giving up, Jesus remains. I won't say he *simply* remains, because I believe remaining is a full-energy effort for us and likely for Jesus too. He could have rebuked the whole situation and claimed immediate relief, but instead he remained in the presence of the restless questions.

We can walk away from this passage and think, "Sure, I'll be more like Jesus in my restlessness. I'll just *remain* in it." The desire to remain is healthy, but the work of remaining is far more challenging than we realize. What if Jesus asks us not just to remain in our restless spaces but also to ask the questions that arise? Remain and encounter all that the wilderness has to offer?

What would it really look like to abide in the restless present tense? What if we stayed in this place, where we can't go home but we can't stay forever? Perhaps the place in between is the very place where goodness and grace rise to the surface.

The point of Jesus's time in the wilderness isn't "look at how easy it is to defeat those restless threats." Quite the opposite. The point is that there is safety and grace within the restlessness to ask the questions that truly and deeply shape us and the Divine is with us. We are not alone.

In fact, the wilderness account in Mark says that Jesus "was in the wilderness . . . and he was with the wild beasts; and the angels waited on him" (1:13). This is a compelling picture of our restless seasons: We sit somewhere between the wild beasts and the angels. We abide—that is, we remain with purpose—in the tension between kind comfort and growling threats.

A spirituality for restless seasons says to us, "Here is a gift to you. Remain with the Divine, even when you are unsettled and irritated. Stay here between the wild beasts and the angels." This is the way of life for restless folks. You'll find that the restless present tense—the unsettled, not the stable—is where transformation really happens.

Within these pages, we will build a hearty spirituality for our unsettled seasons. We will sit together in the holy space between where we once were and where we will one day be. The gift of restlessness is that we dig into the present tense without embarrassment or contrition. When we make our home in a space that seems uninhabitable, somewhere between the beasts and the angels, we see that Spirit flourishes in places where nothing else seems to grow. We find there is something of worth in these seemingly desolate places in between.

Unsettled seasons call for a spirituality that helps us not to panic but to ask the clear and compelling questions that naturally rise to the surface.

A RESTLESS PRAYER

When I began writing this book, I wanted to examine how we press toward action out of our restlessness. From simple boredom to hand-wringing impatience, what do we who walk with the Divine do when pressed into unsettled, irritated spaces?

Since curiosity is a spiritual practice that I hold dear, I also wanted to identify the most basic human questions regarding restlessness. What do we ask when we are fixed in these unsettled moments? How can those questions prompt us to explore our own souls, encounter the Spirit of the Divine, lead us back to the teachings of Jesus, and ultimately lead us into deeper spiritual transformation?

Restless moments drive us to ask the good and desperate questions. When we are restless, we pose the truly human questions—which are, of course, the truly spiritual ones.

Where do I belong?

What am I here for?

Is there enough for me?

Can things be mended?

Will we be protected?

Can we be rescued?

Everything that contributes to and is affected by our restlessness is caught up in the scope of our humanity. To be human—meaning *humus*, or "earth"—means to be literally "inspired," or full of breath. We are all filled with the breath of God, sharing the story of creation where *adam* (mankind) came from *adamah* (earth) and rose, filled to the brim with Spirit. To care for our souls, and to embrace the journey of spiritual transformation, means honestly considering these restless human questions with all the transparency we can muster. When we seek belonging, purpose, provision, healing, protection, and rescue—and when those things aren't where we used to find them—we return to the questions at their root.

I found these very human questions in a very visible place. Each chapter of this book gathers around a question that comes from a particular line of what is called the "Our Father," or the "Lord's Prayer." When his student-friends ask Jesus how they should pray, he responds with those now-famous lines. You're likely familiar with a version of this prayer found in Matthew 6:9–13:

> Our Father in heaven, hallowed be your name. Your kingdom come, Your will be done, on earth as it is in heaven. Give us this day our daily bread. And forgive us our debts, as we also have forgiven our debtors. And do not bring us to the time of trial, but rescue us from the evil one.

This prayer evokes all restless human experience, so it shouldn't surprise us that it appears in nearly every expression of Christianity. Differing voices and languages lift these words on a regular basis—in some cases weekly or even daily—regardless of what doctrines we hold. The prayer ligaments together the restless tribe of humanity.

When we pray these lines, we discover belonging, purpose, sustenance, mending, protection, and rescue. These things are the ground for conversation and partnership with the Divine. How would our restless moments change if we felt the freedom to ask the basic human questions on the tip of our tongues?

When we are in seasons of restlessness, this prayer, and the questions behind it, bring us face to face with our most human challenges. Those human challenges, lived in partnership with and in the presence of the Divine, are also spiritual challenges. The air within each question is thick with beauty, goodness, and transformation if we are willing to investigate it.

AN INVITATION

Having spent nearly three and a half decades navigating my own restlessness, I now feel a deep and lasting invitation to help others live with their irritated, unsettled places. As a spiritual director, I hope to stand at the trailhead of your and my restlessness and point the way forward.

As a father, I sat in that lobby, prayerful and anxious over my own daughter's mental health journey. As a spiritual director, I sit with those who have seen their share of lobbies and doctors, crises and catastrophes, and I hope to help them sit in their own wilderness with the Divine. A spiritual director is someone who creates a non-anxious interaction in which another person can listen to the Divine in the context of their everyday life. In spiritual direction sessions, restlessness is a common theme.

Restlessness with God, self, and others is universal, but that universal gift expresses itself differently in our lives. So I have no idea how *you* will do it. I know that reading a book will neither solve the "problem" of restlessness nor give you easy steps for remaining in it. What I do know is that God—the Divine—is found in all spaces and places. As you read, you'll find my own testimony to this ever-present Divine in the way I paraphrase certain passages of scripture. Taking something familiar and giving it a gentle and contemporary turn helps us see the Divine in new and astounding places.

This book is simply an extended beginning—one that hopefully helps you explore your own restlessness and the delightfully human questions restlessness has to offer. Inherent in each question is an invitation to spread our hands wide in frustration, irritation, and instability. This posture allows restlessness to become a welcome gift. Each chapter ends with a spiritual practice that can help us dwell in our restlessness and find there a gift from the Divine.

A pause here may be helpful to clarify a term. Throughout the book, I use the term *the Divine* interchangeably with the word *God*. Perhaps that has caused you a bit of restlessness already. *Divine* is the word that most closely identifies how I now see the reality of the Creator and Sustainer of all things.

As we wait in our restlessness, we can ask: Will we allow ourselves to be led into the wilderness? What are the questions we find at the heart of our own restlessness? How wide can we spread our arms and receive this gift? And what will be transformed as a result?

A PRACTICE
SEEING YOUR RESTLESSNESS

The first step toward claiming the gift of restlessness is saying what is real and true about it. Find a quiet space and a quiet time to do this practice. Put your phone on silent or airplane mode and take a walk or find a seat where you can spend some uninterrupted time. Take a journal or open the notes function on your device to capture any insights that come.

Here is the question: *What are your unsettled, irritated spaces right now?*

Describe these spaces in detail to yourself. What have you assumed about these restless spaces? As you hear the statement "I can't go back, but I can't stay here," what comes to mind? What have you left behind in this irritated, unsettled time? What are you most uncertain about regarding the future?

After you detail your restlessness, sit with what you've unearthed. Focus on your breathing. Take a deep breath in, then let it out completely. After a few rounds, offer this breath prayer on each inhale and exhale:

(Inhale) *Spirit, I can't go back.*
(Exhale) *Spirit, where are we going?*

Stay in this space as long as you can, paying attention to whatever responses you receive from this prayer.

CHAPTER 2

WHERE DO I BELONG?

Our Father . . .

There was a time when I belonged to West Virginia. The red-orange flush of fall on the Appalachians was the backdrop for my growing and learning the ways of being human. I belonged to the bus drivers who called off work on the first day of deer season. The roads bent like question marks were my well-worn paths, and the many windshield dings from passing coal trucks gave me stories to tell.

The achingly hot church sanctuary where I had my first experience with God became a place of connection and belonging. For a time, my family helped clean the church to which we belonged. I had an encyclopedic knowledge of every power outlet in the sanctuary where I could plug in the vacuum and of every problematic toilet in the building. It wasn't simply a public space. It was a place of familiarity—a place where I walked in comfort and had no question about why I was there. It was a kind of home.

Home is the place we long to go when we're restless. When our faith is tested, we return to a well-worn book or the voice of a trusted spiritual mentor. Home is where we do not have to guess at the location of plates, cups, or mugs. It is where we can ease into that comfortable pair of pants, in a familiar chair, with a dog tucked under our arm. (Or perhaps that's just me.)

But what do we do when, literally or metaphorically, we sell the home and move to a new place? When we cannot go "home" again? What happens when our sense of belonging to God, ourselves, and others feels temporary and fragile? When the church sanctuary no longer feels like home? When a spiritual home feels strange and ill-fitting or when the address, the smells, and the cabinets have changed places and arrangements? At that point, a kind of spiritual homelessness seeps into our souls. Here the restless refrain comes to us: "I can't go back home, but I can't stay here either."

Belonging is perhaps the greatest question we face in our seasons of restlessness. How do I belong when everything around me is changing? Or how do I belong when I'm changing and everything around me is staying the same?

When we cannot return to the home that once gave us light, life, and purpose, we wonder how to remain in the restless present tense. We wonder how to inhabit the disconnection with grace and hope.

AN UPPERCASE BELONGING

Belonging is the story of home that we tell to locate our souls within a particular time, place, and people. Belonging is a story we desperately need, and yet it is often the source of our greatest restlessness.

Writing about her Potawatomi heritage, activist Kaitlin B. Curtice talks about belonging from the perspective of a people who have had their key markers of belonging erased by force, their bodies broken, stressed, and displaced. "The sacred thing about being human is that no matter how hard we try to get rid of them, our stories *are our* stories," Curtice writes. "They are carried inside us; they hover over us; they are the tools we use to explain ourselves to one another, to connect."

To be human and spiritual—to seek connection with God, self, and others—is to ask honest questions about our stories of belonging. It is to explore the reality of where and what we call *home*. When we talk about belonging, we are addressing the heart-level understanding of where we call home and what that home means for our lives. Belonging is the foundation on which we build our lives. It can also shift without permission or notice.

Even so, I believe that we are always within arm's reach of an unassailable belonging. This belonging is not rooted in light associations or detached social networks: "friends" we've never talked to in person, parents in our kid's soccer league, or even someone we see in passing after the worship service. This belonging isn't an easy belonging. It is an inner belonging: a flintier, persevering kind rooted in something divine that we all carry within us.

The kind of belonging to which I'm referring requires a capital letter: *Belonging*. It is the kind of home from which there is no eviction, and it persists regardless of circumstance or location. Author Charlotte Donlon refers to this sense of the word in her book about loneliness titled *The Great Belonging*.

This Belonging is distinct from the lowercase belongings that shift and change throughout our lives. The work we do, the stages within our marriage or our role as a parent, the teams we join, or the political parties with which we affiliate—all of these are smaller belongings. None of them alters or revokes the Great Belonging: the deep, significant home we have in the heart and mind of the Divine.

Christian spirituality reminds us that we carry within us a constant home, an unshakable Belonging. The presence of God is not restricted to places we know and where we are known. We are in the presence of and participating with the Divine no matter where we find ourselves. The psalmist says, "If I make my bed in the depths, you are there." Even in the dark, dying places, we are connected to Mystery. We Belong.

We have access to Belonging even when we are out of our element. Even when we feel as if we are standing on one foot at the edge of an immense precipice. Jesus, the living image of the Great Belonging, says, "My spirit will be with you and in you, and you'll *know* me." This is the uppercase Belonging. No matter what happens in our spaces of lowercase belonging, it does not change the reality of our Belonging.

We are ones created very good, called "beloved" in whom the Divine is well pleased, and given life and freedom by Spirit. We are animated by the reality of Christ at the deepest places. "God declared creation very good!" Ronald Rolheiser says. "This constitutes the original blessing, and, for many Christians, this still constitutes how God looks at us and our world, that is, God is still looking at his creation and saying: 'it is indeed very good!'" We can make our home in that very good Belonging without terms or conditions, and we can allow that Belonging to shape all our lowercase belongings.

So when we grow restless about where or if we belong, we are experiencing the tension between our lowercase and uppercase belonging. That is where the Divine invites us to the gritty work of spiritual transformation. The gift of restlessness is that it helps us distinguish between the uppercase Belonging and the many changing lowercase belongings we experience throughout our life.

So how do we live out this Great Belonging when our small belongings change?

MAKING (AND UNMAKING) THE BED

In the 1950s, psychologist John Bowlby developed a concept called attachment theory. Attachment, a key part of human development, establishes from childhood the foundation for where a person belongs. In Bowlby's research, he found that when caregivers meet a child's needs in a consistent, appropriate manner, it creates a feeling of security and safety in the child, allowing them to explore the world with confidence and ease. Children who don't experience secure attachment are less able to trust and connect in healthy ways later in life.

Of course, the dynamics of our early development are outside our control. We don't get to pick the parents, caretakers, or families who write the first chapters of our stories of belonging. This brand of belonging can be a blessing, a curse, or somewhere in between. This family, this house, this location all become the boundary lines of our way of belonging.

Over time, our sense of belonging changes. Whether through our natural process of spiritual maturity or through external influences such as age, job changes, and fading relational or physical health, we are drawn to *detach* from our previous attachments. We begin to think differently about how we belong to the various worlds we inhabit.

Most of the detachment we experience is simply growth and maturity in action. We move away from home and detach from the place that once gave us our sense of belonging. The neighbors of our childhood are replaced by the neighbors in the dorm, the apartment building, or the new house next door.

We begin to redefine home, leaving the place that gave us much of our identity as children and moving toward new places and people with whom we'll express our belonging. A tension emerges as our sense of home shifts, changes, and in many cases disappears.

Detachment may sound like a negative word, but there is a beauty in the letting go. Perhaps it is more helpful to call it *nonattachment*. "Letting go is called non-attachment, but not with the cool, remote quality often associated with that word," writes Buddhist teacher Pema Chödrön. "This non-attachment has more kindness and more intimacy than that. It's actually a desire to know, like the questions of a three-year-old."

To let go of our previous belongings is to begin moving through a wilderness filled with questions and curiosities. We find wisdom here about God, self, and others but only if we're willing to remain in our restlessness and let it teach us about where and how we belong.

This is what spiritual transformation asks of anyone who accepts the life of Belonging: to become one who attaches, detaches, and reattaches and does so in deep trust of the Divine.

Eventually, we find new homes, new friends, and a new way of being with our family and our faith. We find new metaphors for God, and we reattach to places and rhythms and learn to live in this new way of belonging. This journey of attachment, detachment, and reattachment is a natural part of our growth and maturity. Dr. Renita Weems says, "Detaching from something or someone is the prerequisite for moving, living, and breathing in the directives God has planned and ordained for you."

Dr. Weems describes detachment as pulling all the covers off a bed. We can leave it as it is—bare mattress and box springs gathering dust—or we can cover it once again with sheets and comfortable blankets. We can make it a beautiful place of rest. "In its bareness, the former bed was susceptible to the elements in the room," Weems writes. "Likewise is a detached life. It is open to whatever. It is positioned to be filled and possessed. Yes, it is good to detach, but detachment generates a need for an attachment."

Spiritual practices, like prayer and meditation and reading scripture, are holy engines that teach us to attach and detach as we go. A practice of prayer teaches us to let go of the images we inherited and to imagine new ones along the journey. Meditation and scripture fill this imagination with energy and possibility. These three practices, along with others, confirm that the Divine created our minds with the capability of navigating attachment, detachment, and reattachment with grace.

When we have a sense of belonging to God, self, and others, the bed is warm and comfortable. Then growth leads us to a restless point where the previous attachments fall away, when we feel our story of home being rewritten, and when we know we cannot go back.

So how do we make the bed again? How do we reattach to work, relationships, a faith community, even a sense of self? How do we recover our belonging in the world?

A GUIDE TO BELONGING

Our movement between belonging and Belonging requires a guide. The teachings of Jesus offer us a set of touchpoints. At its heart, the way of Jesus is a way of attachment, detachment, and reattachment. Exemplifying these restless movements, Jesus says, "If any want to become my followers [attach to me], let them deny themselves and take up their cross [detach from safety and comfort] and follow me [reattach to me]."

We are like those disciples, restless to connect with the deeper resonance of the Divine. This restlessness propels us from attachment to detachment and back again, always guided and enflamed by Spirit. This way is not a one-time experience, either. It is more like a posture we take—an open and curious way of embracing the restlessness around our belonging.

When pressed on the central reality of life with the Divine, Jesus teaches us to "love the Lord your God with all your heart and with all your soul and with all your mind . . . [and] 'Love your neighbor as yourself.'" We can speak of this in shorthand as loving God, self, and others. These are broad categories, but they are the key places where we embrace our Belonging and establish our lowercase belongings.

It is important to note that these touchpoints do not answer the question "Where do I belong?" Instead, they help us experiment with the question "*How* do I belong?" The difference is that belonging is never a final location; it is a posture we take toward the world.

A long-term marriage often moves from passionate romance to necessary routines to quiet comfort. The question at each stage isn't "Do I belong with this person?" but "*How* do I belong to this person in this new chapter?" This is a posture of presence.

When we assume the Great Belonging and let it flow into the gritty particulars of our lowercase belongings, we strike a posture of presence. This posture allows us to be compassionate, attentive, helpful, and restorative in all the lowercase belongings because we are channeling that deeper Belonging. The Great Belonging points the way for us to engage with the lowercase belongings. The great teaching of Jesus—that all of life radiates from our loving posture toward God, self, and others—is a master class in attachment, detachment, and reattachment.

As we explore these three touchpoints, reflect on which of these belongings—to God, self, or others—create the most unsettled, irritated reaction within you. In which do you feel most disconnected? Why?

BELONGING AND GOD

As a spiritual director, I often ask new directees two questions: "What is your image of God?" and "How do you think God sees you?" The image of God someone holds tells us a great deal about how a person lives, moves, and cultivates their belonging. This includes both the generative and hope-filled images and the scary, shaming images of God.

We don't get to choose the spaces and people who give us our first images of God. For some of us, early influences give us what is necessary for nurturing hope and grace. They teach us to belong to God, self, and others, and they also whisper the rumor of the greater Divine Belonging in our ear. Bible stories may come on the breath of a grandfather, thick with the smell of apple tobacco from his pipe. I heard who God is from a gentle old woman who served us orange drink and sugar cookies; today, that gentle God is the place of my deepest Belonging.

Yet as I hold space for people in spiritual direction, I hear the other type of story as well: those whose early faith development was filled with judgment, domination, and fear. I know this way as well, from some of the years in my spiritual journey. Some people have learned that God doesn't exist and that religious folks are deluded. Belonging, when we begin with a fearful faith, is tentative and anxious. All of our early spiritual formation offers us either connection points to or distance from Belonging.

Images of God can ground us and give us life, direction, and purpose, which is why we are drawn to them: the images draw us into the grand sweeping arc of life with the Divine, which is well beyond our comprehension. Spiritual director and sociologist Susan Phillips says, "Metaphors and verbal images bridge the gap between the conscious and unconscious in us, serving as vehicles of personal and cultural insights . . . Metaphors help us explore 'what if' and 'how' questions."

Our relationship to the Divine is built on metaphors of attachment. Many of us connect early on with images of God such as Father, Warrior, Judge, Source, or Creator, and in doing so, we find a sense of belonging to the Divine, to ourselves, and to others. We see in ourselves a complexity and an artistry that refer to the Creator. These are the waters that shape and smooth us like a river stone. Yet these images often become problematic and unhelpful in later states of our spiritual life.

For Belonging to truly feel like a gift, we need images of God that are generative, unselfish, and graceful. Without those images, the quest for our true and deep Belonging to God will continue to be a balancing of debits and credits. Put simply, our images of God determine if we even *want* to belong to God in the first place.

No theology, doctrine, or practice can overcome an unhealthy image of God. And we are not often taught that the images of God to which we connect are bound to change over time. Our souls are actually built for this change. The more we come to know the Mystery of who God is and what that means in the present tense, the faster we'll detach from lowercase belongings and reattach to the Divine.

Fr. Albert Haase writes that we outgrow our images of God "like we do our clothes and shoes. Over and over again, we learn never to become too comfortable with our images, as if to suggest that we have captured God or figured God out. God-images are like photographs. They lamely capture in one dimension the most superficial aspects of the selfless, loving ground of reality that we know as God."

Some years ago, a person from our congregation reached out to me and asked to meet for coffee. I had seen Dan on Sundays but didn't know him well. As we talked, he confessed to having a spiritual crisis. I asked him to elaborate, and he told a story of a small group meeting where he had voiced a concern about biblical interpretation. "I just don't believe that Jonah was swallowed by a big fish," he told the group.

What followed was a group critique of Dan's faith, fidelity, and trust in God. The meeting left him feeling unsteady and disoriented, as if he had left home and returned to find all of his furniture and possessions swapped out for someone else's. He felt shattered and small. He asked me, "Can I still be a person of faith and not believe this?"

Dan's question reveals the tension between belonging and Belonging. Deep within, Dan still believed he was connected to the Divine, but that smaller belonging to a community called Christians was now in question.

Have you felt Dan's tension? The path beneath our feet sometimes angles away from the understandings of God and the world that we once had. Now it moves toward a great unknown that appears to get darker before it ever glimpses the light. The ways we once embraced God— the spiritual practices, the theologies, and the deeply held beliefs—feel thin and fragile. To admit to the change feels like depression, but it also feels like abandonment and disobedience.

Restlessness calls us to walk all the way into that season of detachment. To experience spiritual transformation, we often have let go of that thing that once gave us a sense of belonging. We must take the steep, rocky path to new attachments with the Divine.

What came next for Dan was three years of spiritual direction. Together we talked through how Dan could detach from his previous images of God, in which he initially found belonging. God as "one who dictated an inerrant book to people, who then wrote it down" was no longer an image Dan could live with. But to what would he attach next? How do we belong to God when our metaphors and images of God change?

Sometimes restlessness questions of belonging to God lead us from attachment to metaphors to an attachment to Mystery. This has been true in my own spiritual journey. As a child and teenager, I had images of God that I now find completely at odds with the life and teachings of Jesus. Yet those gave me a grounding and a way forward in both my Belonging to God and the little belongings of my life.

God may be *like* a Father, in function—but God is not like our fathers in their various states of health, unhealth, and unpredictability. To say the former *is* the latter is to forget that *Father* is simply a marker when it comes to the true Divine. The thing we can know best about the Divine is that the Divine is ultimately a Mystery.

Mystery cuts through our images and conceptions so we're forced to reckon with our restless questions. John O'Donohue reminds us, "Mystics have always recognized that to come deeper into the divine presence within, you need to practice detachment." Mystery allows us to live freely and lightly with our images of God: attaching, detaching, and reattaching throughout the course of our life. We can do this because we do not worship the images or metaphors. The opposite of idolatry—the creating and worshiping of idols—is Mystery.

Our metaphors are not equal to God. The telescope is not the stars. There is no real growth in worshiping the metaphors, no matter how familiar and even helpful they might be.

BELONGING AND SELF

One of the longest journeys of my life has been toward the acceptance of my*self.* This word is problematic for many people of faith. To correct the destructive forms of selfishness and self-centeredness that we're all capable of, the church has often defined the word *self* as an obstacle to faith.

We somehow moved from the philosopher's call to "know thyself" to various iterations of "detest thyself." Yet Jesus's touchpoint says, "Love your neighbor *as yourself.*" True belonging to the Divine, who deeply loves us, leads us to wonder, "How can I hate what God loves?" In fact, loving and belonging to ourselves may be the strongest force for restlessness in our lives because it feels beautiful and forbidden at the same time.

Staring in the mirror, we see our frailties and failures. Why would we love what the apostle Paul calls, in

Romans 7:24, this "body of death"? Or sometimes our "self" is so wounded by the words and actions of others that we can't believe anything good could come to us. We become receptacles of the abuse and consternation of others.

For those on the margins, this dynamic can be even more pronounced. In her book *Abuelita Faith*, Kat Armas reveals what many children of color are taught: that their uniqueness needs to be minimized or erased. "It's easy when we're fed what to think, what to believe about ourselves, our histories, and God," she writes. "When our identities are programmed, we're not taught to really bring our whole selves to the table. We're taught our own thoughts and hearts cannot be trusted in any way, and thus we live in shame, a widened chasm."

So for a wide range of reasons, many of us neglect the self, either because the words and teachings of others have wounded us or because our spiritual tradition has passed on an allergy to "selfishness."

There is nothing wrong with dismantling certain forms of selfishness, of course. We renovate the world when we can leave behind the kind of selfishness that ignores the pain and needs of others. Yet we move to another poisonous posture when we ignore our own needs to attend to the needs of others. "We are whiplashed between an arrogant overestimation of ourselves and a servile underestimation of ourselves," Parker Palmer writes, "but the outcome is always the same: a distortion of the humble yet exalted reality of the human self, a paradoxical pearl of great price."

Many of the pastors and church staff I talk with in spiritual direction have never entertained the idea that their burnout, confusion, and stress radiate from the fact that they see little worth in loving and caring for themselves. The righteous quest for selflessness leads to soul neglect, which can manifest as irritation, anger, a lack of creativity, insomnia, energy hoarding, and more. They have bought into the idea that selflessness and servanthood are the ways to meet the expectations of their role and fulfill their calling. Yet when the quest for selflessness leads to a dysfunctional detachment from their soul, everyone suffers.

When we embrace this dysfunctional selflessness—the kind that destroys self for the sake of others—we relinquish boundaries. We stop asking whether God might be inviting us to detach from this way of working because of what it is doing to our souls.

The onset of the pandemic forced many people who had been headed toward burnout to confront the reality of their soul exhaustion. With lockdowns and canceled events, many of us suddenly realized we had a family with whom we weren't entirely familiar and that this family was lovely and interesting. We realized we enjoyed walking outside, and we began eating dinners together again. We did not hurry to the events and happenings of others but found new ways of doing nothing. A pace of life emerged, and a way of life made itself known. That way of life was far more fruitful than the frantic scratching we did before things shut down. Then, as the world turned back toward some sort of normalcy, we were left with a sense of self that wouldn't let us return to the grind. At the same time, we had no idea what the future of this self looks like.

We couldn't go back, but what would we do instead?

Belonging to ourselves is a way of loving ourselves. This way of loving ourselves requires us to love *all* of ourselves, from the fit to the frail and from the faithful to the false. Belonging to ourselves includes radical honesty about both the true self at the core of who we are and the false self we show to the world.

How we choose to love ourselves is how we will eventually love others. Some people would injure their neighbors if they loved them in the same way they love themselves. We often talk to ourselves and treat ourselves in ways that would be seen as hateful if we said and did those things to others.

We cannot belong to ourselves when we aren't convinced of our Great Belonging. As a result, some of us who are Christians soften our critique and say, "I'm not perfect, just forgiven." But if we're honest, the "forgiven" part of that equation feels tenuous and temporary.

Into our self-disgust, the revolutionary peace of Jesus whispers in our ear, "Love yourself. You're beloved already."

Can we really belong to our self and love who we are regardless of the specters that haunt us? We cannot undo the past, but we often don't know how to move forward with our sagging, saturated selves. Can we love the parts of our bodies that don't work as they used to, and can we give our vulnerability as a gift to ourselves and to others? Can we see any of it as a gift?

Poet Christian Wiman calls us to retain "that space in your heart that once heard a still small voice saying not so much your name but your nature." Restlessness guides us to this question: How do we belong to ourselves? Can we return to the innocence of heart once again? What if restlessness is an invitation to return to a sort of spiritual innocence, a place before our self-destruction?

BELONGING AND OTHERS

We cannot avoid belonging to others because people are, well, *everywhere* and because, as a species, humans require relationship. In fact, the way we belong to God and to ourselves flows toward the way we belong to others.

Yet we cannot belong to everyone. Many of us need to know who "our people" are—those who know us well in both the universal themes we all share and in our unique idiosyncrasies. So how do we engage the universal in our own specific little worlds? How do we belong to each other?

The best way we can belong to others is to first explore our own loneliness. The darkest spaces in our belonging to others are named *loneliness*. Loneliness extends beyond the playground and childhood into studio apartments and row houses and suburban mega-homes.

Loneliness can be a wilderness, a place where we see our relationships and connections as they truly are.

Before we can belong to each other, Spirit invites us to see where we are disconnected.

"We pay a heavy price for not admitting our loneliness, facing it squarely, and grappling with it honestly," Fr. Ronald Rolheiser says. Loneliness is most dangerous, he writes, "when it is not recognized, accepted, and worked through creatively. Conversely, too . . . it is a tremendously creative and humanizing force when it is recognized and addressed."

Knowing that we have always belonged to God, can we bravely look at our own loneliness and understand what it longs for? Can we let Spirit guide us deeper into our disconnection from others rather than accommodating the pain in destructive ways?

In her article "The Loneliness Project," Kristen Radtke says, "It was only through looking at loneliness closely that I learned it was everywhere, and that it was something we shouldn't turn away from, but listen to. I won't pretend to truly understand loneliness or how to solve its problems, but I do know that by looking at it so intensely, I have come to recognize its value. If we let it, loneliness can bring us closer together. That's why we're built to feel lonely at all."

When we can have an open dialogue with the Divine about our loneliness and remain in it, we have something to give to others. Dwelling in the wild, desolate place of our own loneliness can actually make us free to belong to others in healthy and constructive ways.

A parent gives their energy to activities and nurture while their kids live at home. But as college or career calls young adults away from home, parents often aren't ready for a quiet house. For parents, children may have been central to belonging, but they are not the source of Belonging. What invitation is the Great Belonging extending? When a parent of adult children has more time and energy, toward what way of life is Spirit calling them?

Similarly, people who have worshiped in a local church for a long time may feel increasingly lonely as their theology shifts away from the doctrines the congregation holds or as they watch the church move into a theological stream that makes them uncomfortable. Many of the folks I walk with in spiritual direction have changed faith communities, but many did so long after their theology had shifted. Why? They feared the loneliness of losing their "people" far more than they feared the change in their belief about the Divine.

Belonging to others is always a delicate balance between what we need and what others need. We have limited energy and capacity, but the world around us appears to have unlimited needs. So to belong to others is also to confront our own vulnerability.

Our specific loneliness and disconnection can also create dysfunction of a universal nature. White people, for example, can funnel the specific loneliness or alienation we feel into the destructive stream of racism. Racism is the antithesis of the belief that we are all inheritors of the divine Belonging. Growing up in southern West Virginia, I was surrounded by language and humor saturated with racist imagery. The people I heard delivering these lines were the same people who cared for me, taught me, and showed kindness to others. How do you call out the racism in someone you love, knowing it may fray the relationship? The restlessness around belonging to family, and the fear of loneliness, can hinder our ability to speak justly and truthfully to racism.

If we are interested in true and significant belonging, the invitation from the Divine will be to enter into mystery—not only the mystery of God but also the mystery of ourselves and others. When we explore the loneliness and disconnection from ourselves and others, that land between wild beasts and angels, we begin to learn how to love ourselves well for the sake of the One who created and loves us first.

BELONGING AND SOMETHING BLUE

Recently I was having coffee with a friend. During our conversation, I had one eye on my friend and another on a mother and daughter sitting on a couch, waiting for their order. The mother was holding her daughter's hand. The little girl wore pink shin-height galoshes and shorts with a floral print that declared war on the decidedly different floral print of her shirt. Her hair fell chaotically, framing her face, remaining in place with barrettes. Even though the little girl had an open, curious posture to the world, she also knew this was not a place for her. In this place, the tall people who often missed her or made light of her presence were of no interest. She wriggled and squirmed, and it took little intuition to see that she felt she didn't belong—and the sooner Mom could remedy that reality, the better. The pained look on her face spoke volumes.

I grinned as I listened in on their conversation. "Okay," the mother whispered. "Let's play 'I Spy.'" Her daughter's demeanor changed completely, becoming focused and still. "I spy with my little eye," the mother sang, "something blue."

The child's small eyes darted left and right, up and down, taking in all the contours of the space and searching for something blue. The little girl guessed at blue objects scattered throughout until her mother said, "Good job!"

That coffee shop—a place that had previously held no connection or belonging for her—suddenly became a familiar place. She knew what blue was. If she knew what blue was, then she could find it. If she could find it, then she could know where she was. Color became a way to moor herself to the here and now, a way to belong to this place.

When therapists help individuals with high anxiety, they often ask them to find three or four things around them of a certain color. Anxiety takes us out of the place where we are, removing the marks of our belonging. But finding things of a certain color—blue or red or yellow or green—gives us a sense of groundedness, a presence that helps take the sharpness out of our anxiety. Identifying markers of comfort and familiarity can bring a sense of Belonging in the restless present tense.

Anxiety often results when our deepest sense of belonging is no longer visible or accessible. Sometimes we look around our lives and cannot see "something *God*." When the God of our childhood (either literal or metaphorical) seems distant, our anxiety can spike. We can feel a sense of loss greater than any previous vacuum in our lives.

When we look around and the people who surround us are the same people as always, we wonder how we could belong to a community when somehow their faces are no longer the same. We found hope in who they were, but now it feels like meeting strangers in our own homes and neighborhoods. When we don't know where we belong among the once-familiar crew, what then?

The mirror, the journal, and our kindest friend tell us that we have changed. We have accepted the invitation to detach and reattach—to embrace the restless journey of belonging, knowing our Belonging is never really in question.

And so we keep the lowercase belongings in front of us. We search for colors, shapes, and songs that point to that divine Belonging to God, self, and others that keeps us alive, moving, and having our being.

A PRACTICE
BELONGING IN THE BELONGINGS

Find a piece of paper or a 3×5 notecard. You can also do this practice using your digital device. Whatever your medium, create an image using words or even drawings that communicates: "You belong, no matter what."

Put this card or note somewhere that you will see it on a regular basis. Hang it on the wall behind your computer or on the mirror in the bathroom. If you use your device, make a calendar reminder to consider this statement at regular intervals throughout the day.

As you look at this statement, think also about your restless present tense. Consider the following questions:

1. If I truly belong to God, how do I navigate the changes in my relationship with God?

2. If I truly belong to God, what images of God do I need to remind me of that belonging?

3. If I truly belong to God, where is my first step toward loving myself?

4. If I truly belong to God, what do I do with the evolution of relationships with family or friends that I am experiencing?

Consider including a friend or trusted member of your community in this practice.

CHAPTER 3

WHAT AM I HERE FOR?

Let your kingdom come . . .

Are we really going to get up this morning, wipe the sleep from our eyes, and do *this* again? Coffee revives us, a bit of breakfast and a shower, and then the work of the day begins. Perhaps we wake a child and begin the work of parenting. Or we settle into our job, the papers or computer or conveyor belt or classroom before us. The tasks emerge, whether after a long commute or a short one from the kitchen to the study.

Throughout the day, we hide our irritations, we dote briefly on the joys, but eventually the restless question comes: Is *this* really what we're here for? Is this my purpose?

The question of purpose comes to all of us, albeit in different ways. Purpose is the question of the downsized employee whose dream job evaporated into mist. A new job would allow for movement forward, but all she can see is the restless present tense.

Purpose is the question of the father who suddenly has an empty nest. The hood of the car is now cool where it was once warmed with errands and practices and school pickup. He loved the parental role he once had, and he is not sure what happens next.

Or maybe health challenges have forced us to relinquish activities and movements that once gave us life. So what now? We realize that our job—what we do to pay the bills—isn't what gives us life. Is it possible to find purpose in something beyond our paycheck? The *this* of our purpose shifts and changes, so we must change. But into what and how and where?

Purpose is a searching, longing question. In recent studies, 50 percent of Americans say they are actively trying to "discover" themselves, and around 40 percent say they are still searching for "purpose in life." All those people probably have their own way of defining purpose, but for the sake of a shared definition, let's say purpose is the personal reality by which we evaluate and measure our value in the world.

We often inquire into purpose with a task-focused question: what do I need to *do*? But we can ask a far more probing question about purpose from a posture of restlessness. What if the question of purpose isn't at all about what we *do* but about what we truly *love*?

Love and purpose are intimately tied together in the divine order of the world. And the unique gift of restlessness is that it can dig beneath the question of purpose to the deeper question: what do you truly love?

Restlessness can teach us so many things, but above all it teaches us how to love. If you learn to live in the space between the wild beasts and the angels, you learn also how to give yourself away. You learn the sacrificial way of love by learning to be patient with that which cannot be immediately changed—including other people. Love without restlessness is a love without musculature. Without the strength that comes from restlessness, our love becomes immobile. Without restlessness, love lacks the fortitude to effect change or goodness or beauty in the world.

One way to paraphrase Jesus's "greatest" commandment is this: "Love God, yourself, and others with every fiber of your being." We find the touchstones of our belonging in this passage as well as the singular purpose of humanity. We are loved, and we are here to love. Because we love, the world cannot be the same. The order of all things is forced to change by virtue of a love that paints a different vision of reality.

So no matter what we do for a living, our true purpose is to love and be loved. This is not a job, but it is a posture of the soul. And behind all of it is a still greater, unfolding vision.

To ask the question "What do I love?" as we seek our purpose is to reconsider what matters most. When love is the driver, we think differently about money and accolades. Love shapes how we act toward those we serve: our coworkers, our churches, our families, and our friends. Above all, love reduces our need to grasp and control;

when we are caught up in something beyond our imagination, who are we to control *anything*?

When we are living between these two questions—"What should I do?" and "What do I love?"—we need something to ground us. I believe we need a divine dream.

THE THING BEHIND OUR PURPOSE

As a kid, I loved the playland in our local McDonald's. We would dive face-first into the ball pit—or what I now know as a multicolored petri dish where all forms of bacteria grow and thrive. As children, we didn't care. We climbed the netting and navigated the yellow-tinted tubes. Down the slide, arms up, we descended only to ascend again.

What an ingenious thing, we thought. During my birthday party one year—which of course was held at McDonald's because it was the 1980s—a particularly rowdy guest, we'll call him Jake, smashed a ketchup packet with his hand. Red paste covered my mom's shirt in a salty crimson spray, making it look more like a crime scene than a birthday party. Jake laughed. My mom did not.

But the playland. That place created a joyful space, a particular kind of world we pursued with love. McDonald's was a world for children and early risers, working-class heroes on the way to what came next. It was a place for those down on their luck needing a cheap meal. And at the center of this world, an intricate indoor playground stoked the imaginations of the gathered children with hope, innocence, and, in ways imperceptible, love. We loved what we were doing as we played.

The question of purpose didn't occur to us in the innocence and joy of that moment. I know I loved being there, and for the moment, I loved those with me—even Jake.

When Jesus speaks about the kingdom of God or kingdom of heaven, I believe he had in mind an innocent place where no one really has a job description but everyone knows why they are there. It is a place where small movements—mustard-seed and leaven moments—lead to large-scale transformation. The purpose, then, is to live out the love of being a part of a joyful space: to play, to share (most of the time), to laugh, and to create.

The kingdom of God is a captivating reality, a space that gathers anyone who would want to come and give energy and focus to their loves. Anyone who would want to stop long enough to pay attention is welcome. The kingdom is a deep well of both love and purpose for a wandering people, and in the reality of the kingdom, we learn to live as mortal minor miracles.

Kingdoms aren't the easiest symbols for our contemporary minds to grasp, so perhaps a phrase like *divine dream* is a better image for us. The dream of God—for love to rule and reign within all aspects of creation—is the heart of our restless search for purpose. This dream also serves as the *source* of our purpose as well.

The divine dream is the thing operating behind our search for purpose. It is already buried within us—a nearly subconscious sense of a place, a people, and a way of being that is rooted in love. Not a faraway place but a reality that feels as if it is just beyond our next breath or around the next corner. And we cannot ignore it.

"To be human is to be animated and oriented by some vision of the good life," writes James K. A. Smith. "And we *want* that. We crave it. We desire it. This is why our most fundamental mode of orientation to the world is love."

When we encounter restlessness around our purpose, we are feeling the tension between the divine dream reverberating throughout the world and our desire to put our love into action.

The divine dream seen in the life of Jesus is love made manifest, from top to bottom. The world Jesus shaped in his life and teaching is the playland made perfect, mature, wise, and vibrant. Living in this dream means sitting dead center in divine love and letting all else flow from that. That love is everywhere, unbounded and uncontainable, and it frees us to apply divine love wherever and whomever we are.

As we sleep, we sleep as ones deeply loved and purposed in the divine dream. When we crunch the numbers, have the hard conversation, or pack yet another lunch, we are loved. We possess purpose that alters the world. When we go to therapy and find support for our mental health struggles with honesty and perseverance, again, we are deeply loved and well-purposed. We are part of a wilder dream for the world.

When in the thick of writing and revising this book, scratching my head and drinking numerous cups of tea, I had to constantly remind myself that I wrote and struggled within the divine dream. No amount of bad— or good—writing would change that. I was free to love the words and send them into your experience, open to whatever Spirit would do with these simple characters.

This dream is the reverberating reality underneath territory, people, practice, and time. It's the kind of thing you don't talk about or study; the dream is that which is simply *known* in the gravelly lowlands of our souls. You don't have to tell children how to play in a McDonald's playland; you just have to set them loose.

So how do we choose to live and love as if the divine dream is coming true? How do we set ourselves loose within it?

A WIDER PATH OF PURPOSE

I have the great pleasure of frequently sitting with young adults at the beginning of their professional journeys: as they graduate from college, move out of their parents' homes, and sometimes get married. They often say to me, "I'm just not sure what to do." Even more often, they come with two options in front of them: two different job possibilities, one path of study or another, a relationship to continue or singleness to pursue. The restless wilderness stretches out in front of them: they cannot go back to adolescence, but the way into adulthood appears cloudy and possibly haunted. "I'm just not sure which way God wants me to take," they say.

Here is where the love within the divine dream is so potent. If the dream is fulfilled by loving God, self, and others with everything you have, think about how many different jobs, roles, or projects give you the opportunity to love well!

Those who have a Christian faith background often talk about finding their "calling." In the churches in which I grew up, *calling* was code for God inviting you to be a pastor. It was always externalized—*God* called you—and the idea that calling might be an invitation that wells up from within wasn't part of the conversation. And the calling was never believed to be to become an accountant, or a custodian, or a pipefitter. I also grieve the fact that apparently the very specific call was unavailable to women.

A calling created a higher-class person. In many cases, it also created an impossible-to-escape professional life scenario. Once you were called, there was no turning back.

The path of calling was always slim and singular. Often called *God's will*, the path was a one-time offering that we either embraced fully or missed completely. We were taught that God had one plan for a person, a plan that could be missed if you didn't take the right step at the right moment. If you missed it, you'd have to settle for the equivalent of a divine silver medal.

Many of us bathed in that theology develop significant anxiety around "finding God's will" in every decision, from where to work to whom to marry. Granted, many of us have also used this narrow idea of God's will as a cover to break up with significant others and avert both responsibilities and consequences. But that is a discussion for another time.

I grew up believing that my purpose was to be a pastor in a church until old age or sickness brought me to a final rest. I prepared for this work through college and seminary, and I found life and purpose there. Walking with students and adults in churches both small and large gave me graces I couldn't imagine. Through it all, I believed that remaining in that purpose was an act of obedience to God, and to step out of it was an act of rebellion.

Over time, however, my life circumstances changed. We moved to Chicago, which I didn't know was in the "will." I always thought I would stay closer to my southern roots. My work in churches shifted from full-time lead pastor or preaching roles to a part-time role, and I chose to keep it that way. I could have likely found a full-time pastoral role, and I could have probably found fulfillment in it. Becoming a spiritual director wasn't exactly *un*-pastoral, but it certainly wasn't part of the original plan. Still, as I sensed love inviting me to explore new territories, I found that I could love with all my faculties right where I was.

The deeper love of the divine dream asked me questions that I now pose to those at the beginning of their vocational journey: What if you are invited to choose? What if the Divine trusts you with this decision? What if *that* is God's will? What if there is freedom within this divine dream for you, with all your fears, expectations, and presuppositions, to choose a path based primarily on what you love?

When I say this to people who have inherited the "one-way vocation" narrative and watch their faces, they seem shocked. Afraid. In the face of a divine love that sets us free, we're still often petrified of stepping out of line. If God's will, rather than being a limited and narrow path, is instead a broad spectrum, then it will be filled with ways in which we love the Divine, ourselves, and others with the innocent joy of children.

The human questions that emerge in restless times teach us about our purpose. It is the restlessness around purpose that *makes* us purposeful because it sifts out our true loves. So while our ultimate purpose is to love and be loved, we can exercise the *how* of that love with freedom and creativity.

FEAR AND LESSER DREAMS

The greatest enemy of our restless pursuit of purpose is fear. Finding our purpose means asking the questions that emerge at the intersection of God's dream, our competing loves, and our greatest fears.

This isn't surprising really. "When we consider how much our educational, political, religious, and even social lives are geared to finding answers to questions born of fear, it is not hard to understand why a message of love has little chance of being heard," writes Henri Nouwen. "Fearful questions never lead to love-filled answers."

Love and fear do not play well with each other. Love wants to cultivate hope, risk, and joy, while fear presses in with a fury and warns us of darkness and demons just around the next corner. Love consumes us by filling every available space. Fear chooses a quiet corner and launches incursions against the divine dream sparking to life within us. If we let it, fear can paralyze the divine love that animates us. When we decide to press into love as our true purpose, we will certainly encounter fear. Parker Palmer reminds us of the reality that we "will always have fears, but I need not be my fears—for there are other places in my inner landscape from which I can speak and act."

Fear causes us to choose work or roles based on our desire to preserve our significance. The desire to remain relevant, powerful, and spectacular in our job causes us to engage in unhealthy rhythms of overwork, to skip out on rest or relationships because we want to be known as someone who "gets things done."

I have walked with individuals who fully embraced the performance-oriented mindset that you are what you accomplish. They rarely love what they do, and they often experience spiritual and relational disintegration. Many of them knew the disintegration was coming, but they could not enter into the restlessness of considering alternative ways of living and working.

Instead, they avoided the restless questions and chose lesser dreams, which were easier options than the beautiful vibrancy of the divine dream. The lesser dreams of money, sex, power, security, and ease require so much less of us. James K. A. Smith calls these the "rival liturgies": the habits that form our hearts in opposition to the divine dream and ultimately fail to sustain and satisfy.

Without the tension between the divine dream and our lesser dreams, we would only change jobs or roles and never allow Spirit to transform our hearts. We would adopt a new title but remain unmoved toward what matters most. But when we let our restlessness teach us about our loves, that unsettled season also gives us insight into the divine dream. Where might the divine dream take us if we leaned into loving and being loved as the only purpose that matters? What fears and uncertainties linger at the edges of that invitation?

I believe a voice calls us forward: "You already belong. The question is settled. What might love do in you and through you today?" To turn away from this question is to miss the beauty of transformation. It is to choose a lesser dream, one that is not inherently evil but that falls short of the kind of love that overcomes death. Fear will always be a jealous, malevolent, and manipulative lover. The divine dream will always set us free.

AN ALTERNATIVE STORY

After leading a weeklong spiritual formation retreat in Sydney, Australia, my friend John and I drove several hours from Sydney to Golburn. With rising hills to the east and west and stretches of flat land directly in front of us, we rolled through town until we reached the far border of the community. In the distance was a large red-brick building, perched on a gentle rise and in the middle stages of a construction project. A few trees stood like sentinels at the edge of the property.

I was tired. I had been in Sydney for a week but had yet to adjust to the seventeen-hour time difference. But my energy changed as we drove onto the property. We were to visit a couple, Darrell and Maggie, who had purchased this imposing building, which was an abandoned orphanage, and the surrounding land. A sheep bleated angrily as we pulled into the driveway, and a softened old sun soaked the rooftops as we drove to the rear of the building.

The main building and two smaller wings were connected by a perpendicular section in the middle, fronted by a courtyard that opened to clearing where we parked. In the courtyard we saw plants and flowers, a large cistern, and, toward the center of the building, the front door. Even in the chaos of renovation, the front entryway beckoned, and a warm glow of light leaked through the windows.

Little did I know the sacredness of what awaited us. The door opened, and Darrell, with a headful of strawberry-blond hair and a ruddy complexion, greeted us. "Casey Tygrett! Christ is risen!" he said. I knew at that point something beautiful was happening. Firelight shadowed the porch in the descending dusk, and I seriously contemplated taking off my shoes. Holy ground.

We spent a glorious evening of sharing food around their expansive table. They were brilliant hosts, carried by an unhurried grace and kindness that came both through conversation and through the food they served. Maggie and Darrell told us the story of moving from the suburbs into this new wilderness. Their oldest daughter had died of heart failure due to a defect present from birth, and her death had spurred them to buy this abandoned oasis at the edge of town. Their younger daughter sat across from me as we ate, having recently received a heart transplant to address the same heart defect her sister once carried.

The promise Darrell had made to his oldest daughter before she died was to buy the orphanage for the sake of creating a community. They would impact Golburn, he had told her, simply by being present and offering their energy and space. So they bought the orphanage and opened a coffee shop in one of the outbuildings, with a space for weddings and community gatherings. They also rehabilitated a small apartment with donations from community agencies to house women recovering from heart transplants or heart failure. Maggie's skills as a nurse, as well as their compassionate presence, made all this possible.

After dinner, John and I and another couple who had joined us for the meal sat around the fire talking. Soon Darrell emerged from the kitchen, wiping his hands. "We are going to have evening prayers in the chapel now," he said. "Everyone is welcome."

We followed him down the hallway to the chapel. After years of neglect, a reality against which Darrell waged war on a weekly basis, the chapel was sparse and dusty.

Maggie had decorated the front of the chapel with a simple table, cross, and arrangement of flowers. Six plastic chairs sat on a rug near the front of the chapel, and we took our places.

After Maggie led us in songs from the Taizé community, I read a passage of scripture, and then we prayed together. There, in that simple space, we engaged in conversation with God about the divine dream for the world. The newborn Australian spring had yet to warm, and I was wearing both jackets I had packed. Without heat, the chill was deep and pervasive. Our prayers echoed throughout the exposed-brick chapel. Something very much *other than* was happening as we sang and read scripture and prayed. Something mysterious was being made practical and obvious.

Driving back to our motel later that evening, I thought about the chapel and the people around the circle. I thought about something Darrell said to me: that he no longer feared death. Yes, he feared the absence of Maggie and his living daughter, and he felt the weight of his other daughter being gone. But he no longer lived in the terror of death. I believed him. I could tell that everything he had was God's alone, and while he did not want to lose his life or his family, he trusted God's provision and mercy.

Something vibrant and light but also very strong was in the air in that still-reviving orphanage. Sitting with Darrell and Maggie, I felt that I could not go home and be the same. I saw love fearlessly embodied by people wounded by grief. Yet rather than being caught in an avalanche of cynicism, they were flowing with grace. I saw purpose driven by a divine force of love.

If I learned anything from that short time with Darrell and Maggie, it is that they lived with the divine dream thrumming in their hearts. They were not perfect people, and they were quite content to mention that in our conversations. It wasn't false humility, either. They genuinely knew their faults and struggles, their great fears and their lesser gods, and that knowledge moved them deeper into an intangible reality.

Perhaps you know people who live in that alternative story. They seem to be caught up in a vastly different plot than everyone else. Their goals and priorities are attending to a higher love and a far braver outcome. These people enter restlessness amid so much distraction and so many contradictory narratives. They find their purpose in loving and being loved when so many other purposes jockey for attention and notoriety.

People like Darrell and Maggie—or the person who came to mind as you were reading their story—carry a larger, ultimate story about their identity and reality. Even at the breaking of day, as morning coffee steams against their cheeks, they are already consumed with that deeper and more significant story. They are intoxicated by the divine dream, where loving and being loved is the only purpose that matters.

A PRACTICE
WHAT DO YOU LOVE?

What do you really, truly love? When we are stuck in a restless present tense, knowing that we can't go backward but we can't stay where we are, this question becomes critical. In this practice, you'll need your calendar and, if possible, someone you trust who knows you well.

First, spend a little time in meditation and prayer. Ask Spirit to open your eyes and ears to any new insights that may emerge.

Second, think for a moment about the events of your life that brought you to where you are today. What kind of work, experiences, and choices have led you to the things that you're doing right here, right now? Jot down anything that stands out to you.

Third, look at your calendar. Notice what kind of activities and engagements are part of your day, week, or month. Now take a moment in meditation over your calendar and ask Spirit, "Teach me about what I love as I look at my week."

Obviously, you *have* to do certain things, like paying taxes. But this practice gives you a chance to look at your life as it is and learn from the Divine about how you love well while fulfilling your daily obligations.

CHAPTER 4

IS THERE ENOUGH?

Give us this day . . .

Analyzing the life of your spouse or a close friend can be a bit like doing archaeology. By digging around, you excavate curious artifacts and stories. You piece together where they come from. You discover both the revolutionary and the revolting, and life together becomes accepting the implications of both.

One such discovery began for me with cans of soup. I typically don't spend much time in our cabinets and cupboards. I am more than content to simply find what I am looking for and move on. But early in our marriage, I found myself staring at our canned goods with curiosity.

"Why do we need all that soup?" I asked Holley. We had all the varieties on offer and at least two cans of each.

"So that we have enough," she replied.

"For whom?" I asked. "I mean there are only two of us, and you don't even like that kind of soup." I looked at her.

"We need to make sure we have enough," Holley said matter-of-factly. "You know, just in case."

I let things settle for a while. But a few months later, while packing for one of our moves, I noticed something beyond the cupboard. We had more dishes, more sheets, and more pillowcases than we needed. We had duplicates of our duplicates.

With a keen awareness that Holley could do a similar archaeological dig into *my* way of being in the world, I decided to revisit the cupboard conversation. Our excavations soon led us to her parents. Specifically, it led us to my mother-in-law.

My mother-in-law was the daughter of a Pittsburgh steel worker. The gritty life of a steel man included experiences that many workers know well: strikes, negotiations, layoffs. As a result, my wife's maternal grandmother purchased duplicates of just about everything they'd need from a grocery standpoint. When you didn't know if there would be work in the future, a loaded cupboard brought a sigh of relief. That story—of scarcity and saving and planning for a future of lack—wove itself into my mother-in-law's neural frameworks.

Our brains thrive on repetition and modeling. When we hear a story enough times and then see our loved ones living out that story, it becomes part of us. Faith traditions are so important in part because they shape a follower's brain around a particular story. The result is that we have a comfortable story that organizes our lives, with little thought or effort. What many see as mere rote memorization actually weaves neurological pathways in our brains, creating space for future reflection and understanding of God, self, and others.

It turns out that Holley had *inherited* her way of packing the cupboard. It was a neurologically ingrained way of ensuring survival no matter what may come next. In the first spring of the pandemic, many of us suddenly struggled with exactly how much toilet paper would be sufficient. That season and ongoing supply chain issues took many of us back to a place of warding off scarcity by stockpiling. Even in non-pandemic times, we sometimes turn toward a kind of acceptable hoarding because, well, who knows what might happen? A wise idea in one context ultimately became an unnecessary story for later places and times.

In the years since the cupboard conversation, Holley and I have drastically eliminated the doubles in our cupboard. But we still talk about the "full cupboard principle." We'll notice several cans or boxes of the same thing in our cupboard and say, "Ah, we did it again."

It is difficult to learn how to live at the level of *enough*.

WHAT IS ENOUGH?

Do you have enough?

This question is difficult to answer because we hardly know what *enough* means. The definition can change from person to person and from life stage to life stage.

How much money is enough for someone in their twenties? How much house is enough for a family of three? How much sleep is enough for the parent of a newborn? (The answer is always "*more*.")

The language of *enough* is typically tied to money, but there are other areas of our life where the question "Do you have enough?" best describes our restlessness.

Drilling down, we find another question related to enough: what does it mean to be *content*? When we talk about contentment and learning to recognize when we have enough, we often take aim at those around us who rapidly accumulate *things*. Most of us need only to look around at our own closets and garages to recognize that we are a stuff-drunk culture. Having taken in more than we can handle, we are now at the mercy of the towers of totes and tubs stacked in every available space.

We are spiritually formed by these crammed spaces.

It may seem like contentment is the opposite of restlessness, but I don't believe that to be true. It is when we are confronted with the question "What is enough?" that we have a chance to travel to that unsettled, irritated space. We can find contentment there while waiting with the Divine and learning about what we need.

The search for contentment goes well beyond stuff. We can accumulate friends, jobs, influence, and social media followers. Where is the line at which we say, "I go no further"? Where are we able to say, "This is sufficient for me and my loved ones in this particular time"?

"So much of living is in the wanting, the reaching," author Jedediah Jenkins writes. "I've never loved food more than during a long hunger. And after gorging myself in a moment's rapture, I swear to never eat again." Restlessness launches us into the fray somewhere between "we need more" and "we might have too much." It is in the space between *more* and *too much* that spiritual transformation begins.

The exploration of enough is an inherently restless, human, and therefore spiritual question. Our spiritual lives are organized around stories, images, and memories. In fact, much of our restlessness comes when the story, image, or memory that shapes our world comes into question.

The story of purchasing more than you need because "you never know" begins to shape our will, and we buy two of everything. But what happens when we ask the question "Why do I do this?"

The reshaping of stories, images, and memories is deeply spiritual work. In a sense, this is what Jesus was up to when he taught, "You have heard it said . . . but I say to you."

Much of Jesus's teaching was in fact *rewiring* pathways in his hearers' minds. Their neurobiology had been shaped by stories, practices, and corporate celebrations. He doesn't reject what has gone before; instead, Jesus reframes it. He builds on the previous knowledge and reveals a beautiful way of transformation. The shifting of those stories caused pain, and that pain caused the stalwart religious folks around him to lash out. Their restlessness turned to the fight response and led, eventually, to the cross. This is important to remember that rewiring our stories often means pain and even a kind of death.

When we ask, "What is enough?" we are entering the restless world of transforming stories. We are taking on the stories that we have held dear, whether we know it or not.

So where do we begin in transforming the way we see the concept of *enough*?

A UNIVERSE OF ENOUGH

Creation is not anxious. It is content with its own place, function, and possessions. The pine rests for hundreds of years in its own sustaining purpose. The scrub grass doesn't frantically pace back and forth, wondering if water will soak down to its roots.

As I write this chapter, I'm sitting on the deck of a retreat house in Colorado owned by my friends Jeff and Mindy. They call it the Dream Shed, and they have designated it for dreaming, resting, and solitary creative work like writing. Looking to the right, I see the Flatirons rising like quiet giants. To the left, the road extends on toward Boulder. Pine trees dot every hillside, and scrub grasses and wildflowers roll down and away from the deck. All around me is unhurried, non-anxious creation. Nature is filled with unassuming presence. It is somehow both wild and settled, restless and content.

We learn something about enough as we gaze at nature. Defining *enough* in the way of nature means seeing contentment as fluid and flowing. Sometimes we will have more, and sometimes we will have less. There are winters, and there are springs. The point is how we approach both seasons. Into both, we learn to bring contentment.

Finding enough is a deep dive with the Divine into our identity. The divine dream trades in abundance, not scarcity. Life with God is rooted in the belief that there is always enough of whatever we need. This is an abundance mentality. The opposite—a scarcity mentality—is a frantic scrambling to accumulate and gather, driven by the belief that there is never enough of what we need.

An abundance mentality leads us to a non-anxious posture toward the world. A quieted spirit, a tender heart, open to both receive and give whatever the Divine has in store: that is the non-anxious way. God invites us to use calm energy and unhurried effort in our lives, fueled with thoughts about a universe where pine trees and sparrows never worry about what comes next.

One of the gifts of spiritual direction is that sessions are non-anxious times. We assume that if Spirit meets us there, we have nothing to be anxious about. The directee does not have to achieve anything, and the director need not worry about having enough wise or insightful things to say. The presence of Spirit is the presence of abundance, so we both have what we need.

If we think of the world in terms of abundance rather than scarcity, we can enter the restlessness of both spaces and simply *remain* there. The restless tension here is not whether *more* or *less* is better; it is whether our hearts have a non-anxious posture toward whatever we have.

Once we consider what is enough, can we take a non-anxious posture toward the money we make? Toward our time with our children? Toward what we possess or do not possess? What could we learn if we settled into the space between more and less, listening to our own anxiety along the way?

In 2011, Holley lost her job. Now, looking back, we see it as a watershed moment. The work she was doing had drained her completely. At the same time, we were as financially comfortable as we had ever been—or ever would be again. Strange, isn't it, how certain types of abundance do not, in fact, lead to life?

With the financial implications firmly in place, we did not panic. Somehow we were able to tap into a feeling of freedom and grace. We cut our income by 65 percent, and we felt lighter and more alive as a result. Not every day, mind you. But many days, Spirit met us in non-anxious ways. Even with all the desperate questions, we looked around and noticed that "simple is enough." Without the fear that comes with discontentment, we learned to be creative and hopeful. Then, when Holley returned to work, we asked different questions and learned different lessons. Spirit was giving us a master class in *enough*.

TO BE QUIET AND ALONE

I went to the Dream Shed to cut out distractions and focus on writing. Writing is a turning out of one's soul, and the great enemies of good writing are noise and one's own ego. When I write at home, I'm constantly staving off anxious thoughts about the scarcity of time and the desire for success and sales. The desire for this book to be "the next big thing" is also lurking nearby. Will this one finally be the one that brings recognition? Do I even want that? Is success a good thing? If I do want that, how do I write "the next big thing"? It is very hard in that moment to let sheer creation be *enough*.

There is no such thing as perfection—or fame, for that matter. The point is the faithful completion of what I have been given to do, and I am learning how to be content with that. I want to know that my writing comes from a deep and good place, and so I must believe that the act of writing itself is also enough. I am learning, with every word, to be content with the words themselves and to leave the rest to Spirit. Our anxiety around scarcity is deeply tied to whether we can look at what is and say, "This is enough." The restlessness of a writer is that we write to create, but we publish to be read. I believe God meets the writer for a chat somewhere in between.

While this particular restlessness is part of a writer's life, it likely makes sense to anyone searching for enough. Any of us who longs to cultivate a non-anxious presence in the world needs to turn down the volume and trim the ego. In terms of spiritual transformation, this means seeking solitude and silence. Richard Foster defines solitude as "the inward unity that frees us from the panicked need for acclaim and approval. Through it we are enabled to be genuinely alone, for the fear of obscurity is gone;

and we are enabled to be genuinely with others, for they no longer control us."

In silence and solitude, we learn to dismantle the scarcity mentality and the endless hunger for more. The restless parts of us are the noisemakers that distract us from the divine dream. In silence and solitude, Spirit brings our deep hungers to the surface and unmasks them in front of us. "Are you willing to dismantle the destructive parts of these hungers?" Spirit asks. "Will you stop spending energies that take you beyond enough?"

Silence and solitude are ideal places to wrestle with our anxious thoughts about enough. In fact, silence and solitude empty us of everything *but* enough.

When a global crisis scrambles our economy, our relationships, and our work, it is difficult to stand against the tide of distraction and protectionism. When the noise of self-protection and chaos rises to untenable decibels, we grab the nearest earplugs we can find. A well-placed time of silence and solitude is helpful as we learn to be content even in the middle of the scrambling and the noise. It helps us to hear the Divine when scarcity is screaming at full volume. Thomas Keating says silence "is God's first language. Everything else is a poor translation."

Entering the solitude of what *is*, and being content to remain there, helps us learn about our own restless chase for more. In the quiet places, we begin to see our own craving for more in the way of words, recognition, and fame. In silence and solitude, we are learning the language of *enough* by bearing witness to our discontent.

Solitude strips us of our typical means of approval, financial gain, and the basic act of accumulation. When we move to that place, we can define what *enough* truly means. We can think clearly from a non-anxious space. Like spiritual direction, silence and solitude leave us without the urge to fix or repair or gather. We are alone on the edge of reality, and the only other presence there is God. In silence and solitude, God must be enough. The panic we may feel in silence and solitude is a clear sign of where scarcity mentality operates in our lives. Scarcity doesn't allow us to settle, to rest, and to clear our mind to focus on the Divine speaking to us.

In silence and solitude, you can "recover [your] mind and [your] will which are busying themselves elsewhere," says Renaissance philosopher Michel Montaigne. "You are draining away and scattering yourself. Concentrate yourself; hold yourself back. You are being betrayed, dissipated, robbed."

Even Jesus found the silence and solitude an apt reminder of the way of enough. Through times in the solitary wilderness apart from his followers, he waited in the restlessness. As we wait in our own wilderness, we are reminded to live as the divine dream in human form. There we learn that we are enough. We can enter a non-anxious space despite our restlessness, and silence and solitude begin to repair our hearts and minds. We learn to live with a unified perspective on God, self, and others because of the simple contentment silence and solitude offer.

A NON-ANXIOUS WILL

I often have conversations with people about contentment and discontentment. Whether it has to do with their engagement with God, a great need, or a prayerful conversation they've been pursuing for some time, people often hint at a restlessness that seems antithetical to contentment. I often ask them what will happen if they don't receive what they are searching for. What if what they need or desire doesn't come to them?

Asking this question of others can feel a bit hypocritical because I, too, have often struggled with contentment. Compulsive behavior, not restlessness, is the antithesis of contentment, and I have wrestled with compulsions for most of my life. From attention to food, from pornography in years past to videogames in the present, I have not been the picture of restraint when it comes to enough.

Yet in each of these areas, I have learned a great deal from Spirit about what I truly love. Healing from my compulsive behaviors has required that I understand that every yes is a no. To step into a videogame means I am giving time that cannot be given elsewhere. The value of that time is both minor (hours, minutes, days) and major (creative work, relationships, rest).

Realignment of our yes and no responses is truly a transformation of our will. Receiving the gift of restlessness here means learning to align our will with a divinely sourced abundance mentality. We know this is an experiment at which we will both succeed and fail. Yet we come with energy and hope, partnering with the Divine all the way.

One of the key pieces of spiritual transformation—or any kind of transformation, for that matter—is understanding our will and knowing how we empower it. Our will, Dallas Willard says, is "the ability to originate or refrain from originating something: an act or a thing. It brings things into existence." It doesn't operate apart from our thoughts or apart from Spirit, however. It takes its cues from the things we are already thinking and the wisdom of the Divine flowing through us.

Judith Grisel, writing about her own experience with addiction, says "the opposite of addiction . . . is not sobriety but choice." When we desire a particular choice, our thinking and understanding are converted, and the will—the energy—follows suit. Any non-anxious posture toward the world requires that we engage with our will and make choices rooted in contentment.

Our will is driven primarily by story, image, and memory. So if we have a scarcity-driven way of seeing the world, our will seeks more and more to soothe the savage beast of our anxiety. But if we remember that we are living in a non-anxious story—one in which there is enough for us and for everyone else—we can put our will toward living gently and easily within that story.

Either way, we end up doing that which we allow our will to pursue. We find a home in committing our minds and will to things like the non-anxious pursuit of enough. Joan Chittister says that commitment "drives us on past the pursuit of perfection to a sense of being at home within ourselves."

Jesus tells us, "Let your word be 'Yes, yes' or 'no, no'." This is primarily a word about integrity. But in a universe of scarcity, where you feel you must game the system or manipulate others with your words, there is not enough stuff, time, energy, or personal prestige. The only option is to hoard and scrape and promise all that you can.

Strange, isn't it, that all this gathering and hoarding only leads to a deeper restlessness? Instead, the Divine allows us, in the restless questions of enough, to seek and find the non-anxious spaces of silence and solitude.

WINSTON AND PRIVILEGES ON THE PATH

Every walk with Winston the Westie is a lesson in theology. One day not long ago, I attached the leash for our afternoon walk. When eighty-degree temperatures are paired with nearly 95 percent humidity, it is fit neither for man nor dog.

At a certain point on our route, I had a choice to make. Winston and I could continue north toward the park, following the sidewalks until they turn to wide blacktop paths dotted with goose droppings. Or we could turn south and follow the sidewalk until it ends and then continue through the apartment parking lot to the path through the forest preserve. I chose the southern route.

Winston hesitated, as if he knew the forest preserve path was the longer route. It meant further from home, from his chair, from naps and all things that dogs love.

But the day was glowing, and the time was ours. So we kept walking.

It was just after we left the shade of the trees that we saw her. I saw her first, then Winston. He is a lovely dog but not the most observant. Amazing that his breed originally hunted foxes. He rarely notices the rabbits standing mere feet to his left or right.

In the middle of the path sat a woman dressed all in black, save for a tan leather belt. She sat with her legs crossed and her back turned to us. Her silver-black hair was tied haphazardly into a knot, and a plaid backpack leaned against her thigh.

I said hello as we passed, but she only nodded. She was concentrating on something, giving it her full attention. Her face was soft, at ease, unhurried. The best conversations are those in our own heads, I suppose.

As we walked by, it occurred to me that she was either homeless or facing some sort of housing insecurity. In front of her was a small takeout container full of food. Then again, perhaps this was simply a moment of peace during a chaotic day—or a chaotic life.

As we walked, I thought about this woman, and I wondered whether she had enough. Did that moment of peace satisfy some need, some longing deep in her? As I walked, music hummed from the device in my pocket to the devices in my ears. I walked in a tax-funded public recreation area with little fear of death or physical harm. Was that enough for me? If it all disappeared for some reason, what would I clamor to regain? Or if nothing ever changed, what then? If what I have accumulated already—achievements and accolades, material items and profes-sional advances—is all that is to be, could I live with that?

Winston and I pressed on through the heat, and I didn't look back at the woman. Clearly this moment for her required no audience. Sitting in a forest preserve, a bit of food in front of her, she appeared to inhabit a moment of peace. A sacred time. A moment of enough: enough for her to kneel on the path, and enough for Winston and me to see and recognize contentment.

She clearly lived in a non-anxious universe, where someone else is minding the cupboards.

A PRACTICE
QUESTIONS FOR SILENCE AND SOLITUDE

This practice helps you enter silence and solitude and think about abundance, scarcity, and the concept of enough. Let these four questions be guides.

Find a place where you can exert some control over distractions and where you have limited inter-action with people: a park or retreat center works well, but your car would work too. Thirty minutes or more is ideal to get adjusted to the quiet and to being alone. Turn off your phone.

When you think about contentment, where do you feel irritated or unsettled?

Paying attention to the unsettled and irritated moments of life is critical to understanding the gifts of restlessness that Spirit is bringing to the surface. As you think about the concept of enough in your own life, where do you sense irritation? Where do you feel a need to fix or manage the levels of enough?

What stories or memories lead you to anxiety and discontentment?

This question requires us to be honest about the families and situations that taught us how to assess what is enough. Enter a time of focused remembering: of your own family of origin or of past experiences with times of more and times of less. You may want to journal about a memory that strongly influenced any anxiety you have about enough.

What must happen for you to enter God's non-anxious posture of contentment?

Consider your practices of scarcity: these might include hoarding, grasping, overwork, envy, or the sacrifice of rest. Think carefully about one or two immediate and practical steps you can take in the next week to release some of these. Imagine what it might feel like to live in the non-anxious confidence of contentment.

How can you train your will to live out a new story of abundance?

Leaning into the non-anxious posture of abundance may require that we give things away: possessions, time, relationships, even ourselves. Pretend that you are moving out of your house or apartment tomorrow. As you imagine such a move, ask yourself: What things will *not* make the move along with me? Consider giving those things away right now. If you are willing to part with them tomorrow, then keeping them today likely reflects a posture of scarcity.

CHAPTER 5

CAN THINGS BE MENDED?

Forgive us ... as we forgive ...

Interstate 80 spreads like a great weathered finger across the entirety of the United States. From two lanes to as many as five in some places, the road presses on. Living on the northeast corner of Illinois and having family in northwestern Indiana, I know this path well. I-80 has become a fellow traveler for me, one with an attitude all its own.

On a particularly sunny fall Saturday morning, I made the trek across the state line to Indiana. The radio was on, but my mind was elsewhere. Along with commuters headed to South Bend to see the Fighting Irish, trucks heading to deliver their cargo at a safe (but efficient) rate of speed, I held the pace on the road while I was miles ahead in my mind.

I was headed to have a hard conversation with my dad. This is neither the place nor time to audit what was going on between us. But suffice it to say that the parent-child relationship often lands on strange and uncomfortable ground as the years go on.

We were set to meet at a travel oasis, something I hadn't heard of before we moved to the Illinois-Indiana corridor. Part rest area, part mall food court, the oasis provides a place to make a pit stop and get a soft pretzel, all while suspended above the interstate.

We did not choose the location for the pretzels but for the convenient public space. I don't think either of us expected this conversation to be quiet or nonconfrontational.

As I drove, my mind sifted through the previous discussions. The one with my wife, Holley, after our last hard conversation with my dad. We talked and planned for what needed to be said in this one. I felt a rising discomfort in my stomach, and that tension took my mind from the road and well into the future.

The conversation didn't go well. I said some hard things, and I said some cruel, unnecessary things. Dad returned fire. The wheels came off the conversation, and despite our best efforts, we ended up speaking from a place where critical thinking is nowhere to be found. That is an anxious space—a grasping, needy space.

While I was driving to that meeting, however, I had gotten lost in my thoughts and almost missed an amazing sight. A car had pulled over, its hazard lights flashing. Even from a distance, the tilt of the car gave away the diagnosis: *flat tire.*

Flat tires aren't uncommon. What is uncommon is that the person changing the tire was Hellboy. The character Hellboy first appeared in comic books in 1993. He is a large, red-skinned demon-man with a giant right hand made of stone and two horns protruding from his head, filed down into blunt circles.

And now you have the visual of what I witnessed that day. Here on the interstate was a grown man, dressed in cinema-grade costume and makeup, changing a tire. Something had put the world of tires out of sorts: a busted tube or cracked tread wrecked by a nail or pothole. Hellboy was hard at work mending his world.

What occurs to me now, thinking about that sun-soaked fall day, is that it felt far more believable to me that Hellboy would change a tire on the side of I-80 than that I would make peace with my dad. The rift was so deep and had gone on for so long. What chance was there of going back?

Yet even so, my deep desire was to seal up our fracture and begin the next stage of healing. Forgiveness, it seems, inspires a unique kind of restlessness. To do the work of forgiveness, we live between our desire to see our world mended and the seemingly absurd belief that mending is possible.

BETWEEN DESIRE AND ABSURDITY

Recall someone who has wounded you, cut your spirit down to the bone—someone whose baggage you feel compelled to carry now and forever. The child who knows your weak spots who becomes an adult and uses your weaknesses against you. The hand that should have nurtured you that instead battered you or invaded the sacred safety of your body. The spouse or partner who has shared your joys and trials and who has now left, half the good gifts of those struggles going with them.

Now think of someone *you* have wounded. Those we have harmed are also nursing a wound; they are carrying *our* baggage. Perhaps you spoke a swift and declarative word to a friend with desire for their good but forgot to love or to listen first.

Perhaps you took half the good gifts of someone else's struggles or harmed a child with your harsh and hurried words.

As we think about these scenarios, we probably imagine two different responses. For the wound we carry, we want payback. Watching something marginally painful happen to the one who afflicted pain on us might lift our spirits, we think. Perhaps a smidge of retribution for the harm they caused us would make us feel better?

Yet for the wound that came from *our* hand, word, or deed? For *that* wrong we pray for clemency. Grace. Understanding.

Forgiveness is a concept that gets at the soft tissue of our soul. We all carry wounds, we all wound others, and we all feel the weight of doing something about both scenarios. We tend to believe the Divine puts the "wrath" hat on for the wounds we bear but the "grace" hat on for those we inflict on others.

Nothing makes us restless like the distance between the grace we welcome and the grace we withhold.

Many of our conversations around forgiveness contain the word *should*: I *should* forgive that person, or you *should* forgive your father. In religious terms, forgiveness is the right thing to do, and "unforgiveness" is out of the question.

Forgiveness speaks in a dialect our soul understands. The idea of making peace with another person contains a deep appeal, and the Divine also stokes that desire to mend the world. In the words of authors Jon Huckins and Jer Swigart, "Restoration is what God gave his life for, and he invites us to spend our lives joining him in it."

Yet even with the Divine wind at our back, we are convinced that forgiving that person or being forgiven ourselves is simply *absurd*. This is another time that restlessness settles in: when we are suspended between the wound, the desire for healing, and the belief that healing is nearly impossible. We cannot undo the wound, but we cannot live with it as it is. Forgiveness seems too simple, and making things right feels like weakness. On top of that, we carry a cynicism born of old wounds that never heal into scars.

But ignoring calls and texts will only last so long. Calling in sick and staying home from family events will eventually lead to questions that we cannot honestly answer. At the same time, what good will confronting the rift *really* do?

Like much of our unsettled and irritated experience, sitting suspended between "we should forgive them" and "well, that's just unthinkable" is where we find a gift. God waits between our longing for forgiveness and our cynicism and there speaks quietly in ways that will mend both us and the world.

Before we move much further in this discussion, let me be clear: it is best to undertake the journey of forgiveness in the company of others. Whether you call upon a trauma-informed therapist, spiritual director, or trusted friend, please don't take this journey alone. The mending of the world requires a companion or two.

So how do we live with the unsettled and irritated spaces around forgiveness? When we are convinced that we're more likely to see a demon changing a tire than see the world set right, how do we trust that we will see creation mended and the divine dream come to pass?

TRANSACTION DECLINED

Part of the conflict we feel about forgiveness is a result of what we assume about the nature of forgiveness. When we read "Forgive us our debts as we forgive our debtors," it is hard to see forgiveness as anything other than a transaction. You do this; the Divine does that.

Like a geometry theorem, forgiveness appears to be an "if-then" scenario. If I don't forgive my father or the friend who wounded me, God will leave *my* sins and wrongs unresolved. So taking this phrase at face value seems to suggest that forgiveness is an exchange, a transaction. The addendum to what is often called the Lord's Prayer appears to weave this teaching even more deeply into the give-and-take patchwork: "If you forgive, your Father in heaven will forgive you. But if you do not forgive . . . neither will your father forgive you."

This idea of transactional forgiveness seems damaging, at least to those of us who believe that forgiveness isn't a single act but a way of life. On the surface, it suggests a forgiveness rooted in fear—or if not in fear, then in a minimizing of wounds. Is just one phrase—"I forgive you"—supposed to settle the matter entirely?

In Christian tradition, the crucifixion serves as the apex of forgiveness—the mending of relationships between God and humanity. Many people are introduced to the concept of Christian faith through the vehicle of forgiveness of sins. I do believe that, although the mechanics of the universal forgiveness of sins are well beyond my pay grade. But I also believe that Jesus's death and resurrection are more than an exchange or a formula. As Richard Rohr writes, "Christianity has made the crucifixion itself into a mechanical atonement theory instead of the necessary message of transformation, the price of all true love."

Transactions are easy to define and measure, but spiritual transformation isn't something we experience on a weekend. It is a way we live with the Divine, ourselves, and others in the world over time. Forgiveness is one of the many steps along that transformational way.

The story of forgiveness is like a multi-act play, with tension and conflict in abundance. The deep work of transformation often happens in the restless space between the acts. The first act is the decision to forgive, and what follows is our recommitment to living within that for-giveness. The play then develops incrementally, day by day. We navigate the little setbacks where we reclaim our anger and bitterness toward the person who wounded us. Or our guilt resurfaces over wounds we inflicted on others, and we spiral into shame and self-destruction. Then sometimes the play reaches a climax, and we lock arms with the Divine to mend our little world.

This drama is extensive. Forgiveness is neither simple nor quick. So if forgiveness is not a transaction, how do we pursue the mending of our world?

UNPREDICTABLE MENDING
In more than twenty years of work in faith communities and in spiritual formation, I have yet to see a mending moment of forgiveness that proceeded as I had predicted. There is no method, no map, and no plan for the way forgiveness is supposed to move forward.

Jesus says, "Love your enemies," but he does not give a blueprint on how that sort of work gets done. I imagine if pressed on the *how* question, Jesus may have said, "Well, it really depends on your enemies. What does love look like for your enemies?"

For example, what if our enemy is God? We have been disappointed or felt disenfranchised by the Divine. Can we forgive God? Is entering a posture of forgiveness *toward* the Divine one way to mend the world?

Or what if the greatest offender of our souls is *ourselves?* We are often thrust back to the fundamental structures of who we are. When we walk deeper into our heart's abandoned attics to search out the things that inspire our actions and shape our view of the world, we often find self-hatred and self-wounding. We fail at an assignment, a relationship, or a conflict, and forgiving ourselves appears impossible. How do we forgive ourselves after all that we did to that person, or all that we failed to do, or all the times we broke promises to ourselves? What happens when *we* are the enemy in the "love your enemies" scenario? When we are the enemy we are called to love? How do we forgive ourselves?

The Divine walks us through that space. With the poet of the Hebrew Bible who says, "Search me, O God, and know my heart," we say to God: Walk into the depths of my will, and let me sit there with you. Look at the wounds I've so carefully cultivated and refuse to relinquish. I hold on to them because I don't know how I would live without them.

As we abide with the Divine in this place—the place of our greatest wounding—we realize that we often ignore forgiveness not because we lack desire but because forgiveness is far too *wild*. Our wounds have become comfortable.

A POSTURE

I think differently about my relationship with my wife than I do my relationship with my wireless company. My wireless service provider offers me service of relative quality, and I'm able to use my phone with relative ease.

Were I to "sin" against my wireless company by not making a payment, they might show me grace once or twice, but anything beyond that would sever our contract. The same is true if they were to begin to offer subpar service. I might suffer along with it for a while, but soon I would be looking to part ways. But there is no growth in that relationship—no development, no transformation flowing through our interactions.

With my wife, it is an entirely different scenario. We are both ever-growing souls, in covenant relationship with each other, the Divine, and the world. When I wound her or she wounds me, we grant forgiveness—and then we must learn to live within the ripples of whatever we had done. We are always growing, always attentive to learning from the wounds of the past.

Too often, we think of forgiveness as a contract with a wireless company rather than a way of life we cultivate with another person. Of course, when we forgive someone, we may not be safe enough to maintain a relationship. Sometimes forgiveness leads to relational reconciliation and a return to being in the presence of a person who harmed us. Often it does not—and should not. To forgive an abuser is to know that their words or fists came from painful places of their own cultivation or history. But forgiving an abuser does not mean returning to the line of fire.

It is our posture that makes the difference between living out forgiveness at a distance and forgiving but then reentering danger. The required posture comes from a heart and soul that leans toward the mending of the world. My wife and I do not simply "forgive" each other; we live out forgiveness by not seeing each other as constant enemies.

At one point in the gospels, Peter, one of Jesus's disciples, comes to him and asks, "Lord, how many times shall I forgive my brother or sister who sins against me? Up to seven times?" The depth of this question comes from the ache of Peter's soul for the divine dream. As the story goes, Peter has surrendered everything—job, home, family, and honor—to chase the way of Jesus. I wonder if his question has a very personal grounding—perhaps a restlessness about a wound that lingers, one he has received or inflicted. I wonder if Peter is living in a state of hurt that is both comfortable and uncomfortable at the same time.

Perhaps it was a hurt inflicted on him by a friend or maybe even one of the other disciples. Considering the full and beautiful teachings of Jesus, Peter knows he cannot go back to letting that wound fester. But the questions remain: How many times should I put up with this? When can I remove myself from this way of mending? How many times do I enter the breach and grant release? What *counts*?

Jesus's response is potent and filled with absurdity, at least to his hearers: not seven times, he says, but "seventy times seven." Constructing a 490-point plan toward forgiveness may seem like an adventure in missing the point. But Jesus chooses a perfect number in Jewish thought (seven) and multiplies it by an extreme amount for the purpose of rhetorical force, not dogma. The number 490 indicates not an endpoint but a way of life. His words invite Peter—and all of us who are recipients of forgiveness and grace—to a lifelong posture of forgiveness and grace.

How unsettling is it to think of a life of forgiveness that goes exponentially further than our expectations? Yet forgiveness beyond our expectations is the thing that speaks most clearly to our restless present tense, forming us for a lifelong journey of forgiveness.

Forgiveness isn't a single act but a posture through which the world is mended. Our single acts of forgiving others or seeking forgiveness for ourselves, put together, constitute a way of looking at everyone and everything around us.

The Divine welcomes us, in our restless desire for the world to mend, to take a posture of forgiveness rather than simply fulfilling a contract. We grow as we forgive, and those we forgive have an opportunity to grow as well.

This is how forgiveness is meant to work: By reproducing itself. Forgiveness begets forgiveness. Forgiving and being forgiven give us the health and energy to work toward repair of the world around us. Mending the world within us is how the divine absurdity of forgiveness mends the world around us.

POSTURE PRAYERS

It takes time and practice for us to maintain a posture of forgiveness. The ever-present potential of being wounded makes it difficult to maintain this posture simply by effort. However, holding a phrase or idea in our minds will, over time, allow us to more easily live within the truth of that idea.

In the case of forgiveness, two phrases from scripture stand out. The invitation here is to bring these phrases to mind on a regular basis throughout your day. Used as a breath prayer, where we breathe in while repeating the first half of the phrase and exhale while repeating the second half, these phrases become portable training exercises. They shape our restless minds to assume a posture of forgiveness.

"FORGIVE US... AS WE FORGIVE..."

At the core of this phrase is a beautiful invitation from Spirit to a life of forgiveness. In my work as a pastor and spiritual director, however, I find it is also troubling for people. As we saw, this verse has the potential to limit forgiveness to a conditional transaction. More than that, the conditions are difficult to meet, given that forgiving others is often a lifelong journey.

I don't believe this is meant to be read as an easy interaction or exchange. Instead, if we see this phrase as the invitation to a life, we start to understand new realities about where a wounded world and the divine dream intersect.

"Forgive as we forgive" reminds us that the universe is tilted toward redemption. Grace is oxygen to all of us, should we choose to inhale.

The posture that brings about this kind of mending is not an act but an *address*. To forgive someone—or many someone's—is to abide in a land of ache, beauty, and frequent disappointment. It is a place of work and persistence, not a one-time display of obedience. It is the place in between, the restless present tense. But much like Jesus in the wilderness, we are not completely alone or abandoned. We belong. There is a purpose. We continue to love and mend, as absurd as those things may seem.

The Divine is in the forgiveness business, and so when we take a mending posture toward our world, we are in the presence of grace well beyond what we could imagine. In the words of Dag Hammarskjold, "Forgiveness is the answer to the child's dream of a miracle by which what is broken is made whole again, what is soiled is again made clean. The dream explains why we need to be forgiven, and why we must forgive."

This invitation to "forgive and you will be forgiven" is a call to be drawn to the heart of making broken things whole again. The true desire of Jesus, reflecting the will of the Divine Source, is the restoration and reconciliation of all things. "Behold, I am making all things new," God whispers in Revelation 21:5, as goodness and beauty are rebuilt in a dream of the future.

"FATHER, FORGIVE THEM; FOR THEY DO NOT KNOW WHAT THEY ARE DOING"

These words of Jesus from Luke 23:34 are radical in the sense that they widen our perspective on both our wounds and those who wounded us. The restlessness of forgiveness is important here: we are unsettled by the possibility that grace will open the door to future wounds, but we are just as unsettled by the possibility that others will not extend that grace to us.

To forgive already feels unguarded, vulnerable, and unsafe. We are basically boxing with our guard down, knowing quite well the other person wants to win and will take our defenseless posture and use it against us.

And yet to meditate on this line is to know that there is a subterranean strength to forgiveness. It cuts across the grain of expectation and utilizes a form of power that comes from humility and grace. To truly forgive is to believe there is enough safety and protection in God to grant grace where we would rather enforce the boundaries of anger. Forgiveness prompts us to decenter our ego and our need for vindication, believing that true vengeance offers no return on investment. Instead, we can try to step into the place of our enemy and see the world from their perspective.

Instead of using forgiveness to keep someone at a distance, this phrase also reminds us that what is present in others who wounded us is potentially present in us as well.

How often do we wound because we know no other way of dealing with fear, anger, and hurt? Are our wounds a result of that same confusion on the part of another?

FINDING HUMILITY IN THE HURT

One Christmas season we were strolling around downtown Chicago. One stretch of Michigan Avenue is typically populated by tourists and high-dollar shoppers, but at Christmastime, many others are drawn by trees in the medians drizzled with lights and bright displays in each store window.

At the east end of Michigan Avenue is a courtyard. Trees climb high against the edges of the sidewalks, creating a cobblestone sanctuary just paces from the hustle and bustle. As we approached the courtyard, we heard a voice screaming through a megaphone. We moved closer and saw a fundamentalist religious group screaming condemnation at the gathered crowd. Their judgments ranged from believing in Santa Claus to women talking in public and wearing pants. Every sign they held contained a verse from the Bible.

As we approached, one of the faith aggressors called out my wife for wearing jeans, citing her disobedience to scripture for wearing "man britches." Holley laughed out loud because that's what the comment deserved. My daughter, three or four at the time, sat still in her stroller and watched the chaos unfold.

Typically I walk away from street preachers, shaking my head. This time I didn't walk away. I approached one of the main barkers and tried to engage him on several issues of theology and biblical interpretation. Throughout the whole conversation, Mr. Barker recorded me on his phone. While I tried my best to invite him into a deeper, calmer conversation than the rants and screams, Holley started talking to the other onlookers. "Is your husband one of them?" someone asked.

"No, definitely not," she replied.

"Good," the woman commented as she walked away. "I wouldn't want to be a part of anything those people are selling."

We walked away from the street evangelists, and I felt the anger building in me. For all the crowd knew, this was the whole of Christian tradition at full voice. If this was Christianity, of course the onlookers would want nothing to do with it.

Now, years later, I realize I need to grant some forgiveness to Mr. Barker and his crew. They were operating from a story of condemnation, not compassion. Their cognitive maps of reality said aggression, misogyny, and public derision are the ways to mend the world. They were wrong, of course. They were damaging others. But perhaps they didn't know another story to tell.

I have been the recipient of personal, spiritual violence, and I know it shreds a person from the inside out. And I do not doubt that many wounds come from very intentional acts. We hear the phrase "Forgive them; they don't know what they're doing," and we object, "I believe they knew *exactly* what they were doing." Perhaps they did. I know there were times when I knew my actions would wound someone and went forward regardless.

In Jesus's death, at the height of betrayal and injustice, he utters a phrase that bears reflection. It is easy enough to hear "Forgive them . . . they do not know what they are doing" and dismiss it as just the final act of grace from the eternally graceful person and therefore beyond reach for most of us. At the point of execution, after a rigged trial and unjust sentencing, most of us would hope the whole place burned down as we made our brutal exit. We might prefer the end of the story of Samson to the story of Jesus.

But Spirit empowers us for postures and actions that seem beyond our ability. When we align our will with grace, we are given freedom to act in grace.

There is a gift in this phrase "they don't know what they're doing." Much like "forgive and you will be forgiven," this phrase is an invitation to gain wisdom about what is really happening in seasons of wounding and hurt. Forgiving honors the fact that we are all living from restless stories, images, and memories that have varying degrees of truth and beauty to them.

Restlessness invites us to not only forgive but to see the sacredness within even those who wound us. J. P. Newell points toward the "essential sacredness of all that is born, not only of our lives but the lives of those whom we find it difficult to like or respect."

SACREDNESS AND GARBAGE

It is easy enough for me to point Jesus's statement from the cross at others: "Forgive *them*—you know, Mr. Barker and the like—because *they* don't know what they're doing." Yet living in the rhythm of forgiving and being forgiven means I also must admit that my own ignorance has the potential to wound and destroy. Thich Nhat Hanh puts it this way: "I recognize that there is garbage in me. I am going to transform this garbage into nourishing compost that can make love appear."

Recognizing that the garbage in others mirrors the garbage in me is a humbling move. Humility is like the tiniest seed, planted in a deep, dark universe of dirt. We become just a bit humbler when we realize that we don't know what we're doing—when we realize that the stories, images, and memories we live by have the potential to create both immense beauty and indescribable pain.

We can personalize Jesus's prayer from the cross: "Forgive us, for we don't know what we're doing" or "Forgive me, for I don't know what I'm doing." Meditating on this prayer has a way of transforming our character through releasing our ego. Restlessness peaks when we start messing with the ego because the ego is often what has sustained us thus far. Ego tells us that we are correct and all others are wrong—and *good luck to them*. Though our ego goes with us and can be an important aspect of both early human development and later self-respect and agency, it should not be allowed to govern our lives.

We are all living stories that have dueling potentials. We must take the posture of forgiveness because in our own ignorance, we will eventually wound others as well.

And in turn we remember the world needs mending, regardless of how or why it was torn.

A PRACTICE
TO WHOM IT MAY CONCERN

Writing a letter to someone we have wounded or someone who has wounded us allows us to explore the restlessness we feel about forgiveness. We can be direct and clear when we make time to find the words for how we feel. You may never deliver this letter, but as a work of the heart, writing it may begin the movement toward mending.

Try to write your letter with little attention to decorum. Profanity, anger, and any raw material is appropriate. Often, we don't know how we really feel or what we really think until we write it down, so the full transparency of this letter may be an opportunity for Spirit to lead you into some new insights.

Write with as much detail about the wound or wounding as you possibly can. Again, a therapist or spiritual director can help you carefully enter this practice. You may have to work in bits, allowing the process to linger as far as you are able to tolerate it.

Finally, make a living statement of forgiveness. Use phrases like "Today, I begin the work of letting this wound heal" or "I ask you to begin the process of forgiving me." The letter is a statement of a daily intention and posture. This is the intention of Jesus in asking the disciples to pray into a daily reciprocation of forgiveness. You can include your living statement of forgiveness in the letter if you choose.

Forgiveness is a lifelong posture. This practice of writing a letter to someone you have wounded or who has wounded you is a courageous and earnest beginning and one that's in league with Spirit.

CHAPTER 6

WILL WE BE PROTECTED?

Lead us not . . .

Safety and protection are key to our development as children. Without them, we struggle to take necessary risks in the world. Much like the early attachments we form with parents and caregivers that help us develop, an early sense of safety gives us an innate courage for the life that is to come.

When my daughter was young, she had a habit of running her hand up and down electrical poles. At that time, we lived in an older neighborhood where all the electrical lines remained hoisted above the roads and homes. Each electrical pole was a thick wooden column that smelled faintly like tar.

On our way back from the park, she would run her fingers up and down the surface of one electrical pole after another. "Don't do that, sweetheart," I'd say. "You might get a splinter." She became more secretive over time, only touching an electrical pole when I wasn't looking.

One day on our way back from the park, I heard her cry out. I didn't even need to look at her anguished face to know what had happened. As quickly as I turned to my child, I had to turn my head away. This was not an ordinary splinter. It was an extreme splinter. Later I would wonder aloud to Holley how the pole was still standing after losing that much wood to our daughter's finger.

As any parent knows, to remove a splinter is to court charges of torture. Before the pain can end, it must increase. The skin would need to be pulled back, twee-zers applied, and eventually the splinter would slide free. It meant pain—extreme pain, in the definition of youth. And we all want to be protected from pain, whether it comes from an outside force or is the kind that we inflict on ourselves. In this case, caring for my daughter meant that I, the protector, had to become the threat.

So what happens when we encounter unsafe and unprotected moments in life? And what if those moments actually have the potential to heal, rescue, and restore us?

LONGING FOR SAFETY

In 2020, many of us began to examine what it means to feel safe. During a global pandemic, safety became a deep and abiding question. My mother-in-law has a signifi-cantly compromised immune system. Was it safe for her to be around us at all? Holley would come home from the grocery store with enough supplies for a few weeks. Would it be adequate? We sat all the groceries on a towel in the hallway and wiped them down with bleach spray. Would that keep us safe from the virus?

Our restlessness around safety leads us to take protective measures. And protection typically revolves around threats from the outside—the *that* or the *they* or the *them*—that present as a menace to our lives and our families. The unsettling part of our longing for safety is that we have plenty of examples of times that all the best-laid plans did not work.

But sometimes *we* are threats to ourselves, in our various preoccupations and struggles. Sometimes we need protection from ourselves. In either case, our longing for safety is always rooted in a sense that though we are cared for by the Divine, our immediate circumstances brim with threats to our minds and bodies.

In late 2020, in pursuit of some kind of safety, I began a relatively unintentional project of self-protection. After the mental health challenges our family had faced, the stress and strain of the pandemic, along with health and vocational challenges in early 2021, I began to hide myself away.

I hoarded my energy and my time. Lingering pandemic restrictions made this easy to do. Emotional hoarding—in which we hold back from relationships and conversation because we're afraid our emotional tank may be drained—is not uncommon. I even resisted texting people, as I wanted to conserve as much of my emotional energy as I could and feared I wouldn't have enough for my closest family. While I didn't gain excess weight during the pandemic, I did dive far too deeply into mobile videogaming—anything to distract me from the unsafe, unstable present.

Safety is often seen as an absence of threat. But the temptations to indulge in self-destruction are often just as strong (if not stronger) than those coming from outside sources.

My pandemic safety plan was not without benefits, I admit. There is a time for withdrawal, whether it is a regular time of solitude and silence or the full-on season that comes with major changes or crises in life. Author Katherine May calls these times "wintering": seasons in which we go into hibernation to recover our lives.

As Richard Rohr says, "If you've confronted some hardness in society, some evil in the world, some intransigence in the church, then you have a reason to retreat and gather your inner strength. A lot of spiritual energy is stored in several places: loneliness, silence, and fear. You can find that energy by going there and staying there."

After a global pandemic, leadership and abuse scandals in many churches, and a contentious political season, I looked for energy in less-than-ideal places like social media. Perhaps you did as well. People with compulsive behaviors *really* know how to do self-protection. We find an immersive activity, whether healthy or unhealthy, constructive or destructive, and we take a deep dive.

But does emotional hoarding further the work of loving God, self, and others well? Or is it a way we give in to a temptation—namely, the temptation to mistake safety for ease and comfort? With this temptation in mind, is safety even possible? Or is our restlessness toward safety simply a semaphore—a sign—of something far greater? Something riskier and yet lovelier than we might imagine?

WHAT IT MEANS TO BE SAFE

Defining the word *safety* can be as difficult—and as necessary—as defining a word like *enough*. For some, *safety* means no hassles and problems. It is a life where everything goes smoothly. For those in neighborhoods of violence, safety may mean the kids coming home from school without being shot. For those of us who wrestle with addiction, safety means the right people and protections in place for when we struggle. Safety for a woman or a child who is abused means distance from the abuser and at least one person who says, "I believe you" when they talk about their abuse. Safety for Black and Brown people might look like going to the grocery store or church or downtown without worrying about whether a police officer or a white person with a gun will decide they don't belong or look suspicious.

Safety is deeply linked to feeling protected. When we feel unprotected, unguarded, and vulnerable, we become restless, eager to change our circumstances or location and seek shelter. Regardless of our definition, whatever we consider "unsafe" creates a sense of restlessness within us. Threats to our safety—real or imagined—push us to say, "Something has to change."

What we learn from restlessness, though, is that it is often in the unsafe place—the wilderness place where hunger, loneliness, and even death tease us—where we most frequently meet God. Author Leighton Ford says, "So it may be after some great cataclysm, when we are searching for security and direction, that we are more attuned to listen for God's voice, perhaps because we are shocked enough to stop and listen."

In unsettled moments, when we boldly ask, "Is there protection?" we interrogate our own definitions of safety and our temptation to preserve that safety at all costs. Is it possible that we have missed out on spiritual transformation because we've avoided places that shake us and even feel threatening?

One of Jesus's key teachings alludes to the seemingly unprotected way of grace. When Jesus teaches "I am the way, the truth, and the life," he is making a statement that is well beyond a statement on the exclusivity of the Christian faith. To see these words in that way is actually a distraction.

If Jesus's life and teaching truly embody the *way*, *truth*, and *life*—what we might also call *reality*—then whatever we see in Jesus's life is an articulation of what it means to be human. The spiritual life includes suffering, betrayal, and hardship. Jesus's life embodied the experience of these very human realities.

Being truly safe in the way of Jesus does not mean an absence of suffering. In fact, protecting ourselves from suffering looks like avoiding the painful removal of a splinter: we are not free to thrive. "What would life be like if there were no suffering, no pain?" asks Howard Thurman, who is sometimes known as the spiritual architect of the civil rights movement. "The startling discovery is made that if there were no suffering there would be no freedom . . . Freedom therefore cannot be separated from suffering. This, then, may be one of the ways in which suffering pays for its ride."

In a recent conversation, a friend and I talked about the way Jesus revamps our story of God. The life of Jesus shows us that God becomes *one who can be betrayed*. Betrayal is a distinct act of suffering that only happens when we've opened ourselves up to it. If God can be betrayed, why do we assume we're exempt? In the words of the Mandalorian, "This is the way."

Trying to find safety by our own means can be a way of engineering a reality in which we deny the path, reality, and life force in which God challenges us to live. As we've seen in earlier chapters, the desire for possessions and financial comfort insulates us from the beautiful gifts that come from radical generosity. When we avoid the vulnerability of forgiving someone who wounded us, we miss out on the strength that comes from releasing our ego.

It is possible that we learn to worship the measures of safety with more ardor than the way of the Divine.

Of course, that doesn't mean we don't take wise measures for the sake of safety. Wearing a seatbelt, locking the doors to your house, saving money for an emergency fund: these and other wise steps fit the gift of reason that the Divine has wired into us.

But as John Huckins and Jer Swigart say, if we chase Spirit, we are following "one who moved toward rather than away from potential violence." They add, "We're convinced that our desire to affirm . . . 'security at any cost' rhetoric is a temptation to worship the idol of safety."

OF COURSE

There is no completely safe spiritual journey. A journey of growth and transformation is, by definition, filled with risk and vulnerability. Brené Brown describes vulnerability as "uncertainty, risk, and emotional exposure. But vulnerability is not weakness; it's our most accurate measure of courage." Unsafe places are often the catalysts for renovating our character because they teach us the courage within our vulnerability.

The concept of *shalom* is a helpful idea here. The Hebrew word *shalom* is often translated "peace": but it is not the absence of trouble, it is the presence of order. *Shalom* is peace in which both ease and comfort as well as trouble and trial have their place. It is a radically transformative kind of peace.

We are all changed at the core of our being when we meet the Divine in that place between protection and risk. Transformation begins when we define safety not as the absence of risk but as the restless space between protection and risk.

Secure in our Belonging, living in a universe of abundance, we are set free to risk. Spiritual transformation moves us from believing life is the sum of the five feet around us and into a more eternal way of seeing.

As Brian McLaren says, "Yes, this life has been sweet, and we have practiced—with every breath and pulse and choice—the preserving of our life. But when the time comes to join God in a kind of life that doesn't depend on hearts and lungs and hands and brains, then we let go of this life with God that is known to us so we can join God in that life that is not yet known to us."

Many Christians have struggled with the idea that both trouble and triumph are key aspects of safety. The restless question "Is there protection for me?" is best answered by asking another question: "Does my view of safety mean that I am cared for by the Divine, regardless of what threatens me?"

Fr. Richard Rohr is fond of the phrase "everything belongs." Short phrases and generalizations like this can be helpful as we remain in the tension of restlessness around safety. I've taken that idea of everything belonging in several different directions in the last few years. I developed a way of saying "of course" as a mantra for events that made me uneasy or unsafe. It's a way of preparation that allows me to stay in the restless place between protection and risk. I'd say "of course" to cool my outrage and reset my assumptions about God, myself, and others. It is a way of acceptance—not resignation—that sees the world as it is and, counterintuitively, sees unsettled spaces as normal. It is much easier to stay in a space you learn to expect.

"Of course," I would say when I read the text message from one of my supervisors, accepting the possibility that today would be the day I got fired.

Of course people who tethered their faith to a particular political candidate would break the convictions of the very faith they sought to preserve in order to propel their candidate forward.

Of course systems bent on wealth and comfort, built on the suffering of generations of Black and Brown people, would do whatever it takes to avoid confession, repentance, and restitution.

The mantra "of course" was a way of waiting between safety and the unchecked outrage that was forming in my heart and mind. This phrase helps me learn from Spirit how to respond to vulnerable moments with love instead of outrage or despair.

That is what safety means: to engage the troubles and restlessness that comes with them not in surprise and irritation but in compassion and patience. The mantra "of course" comforts me because it roots me in a God whose outrage slips quietly into grace and peace.

Participating with Spirit in both triumph and trial, we are invited to enter our restlessness around safety and grow into a hearty new understanding of what protection really means.

In the story of Elijah, we find a restless moment suspended somewhere between protection and risk. The prophet is exhausted, having come into conflict with the priests of Baal and a power-mad queen. He runs from everyone and everything. Coming to terms with his frailty, Elijah runs to a wild place. A wilderness. A broom tree reaching into the sun-kissed sky forms shade for his weary body, and, as the story goes, the ravens feed him in between his long periods of sleep.

Napping in a desolate place with ravens delivering takeout may not seem safe. Yet that is where restlessness takes us: between the wild beasts and the angels.

And in that place, the Divine arrives and asks, "What are you doing here?" That seems like a tremendous question for our souls in restless times. When we feel like our cover is gone, through our own faults or through the threats outside of us, we ask ourselves, "What are we doing here?" God may even ask us the same question, not out of accusation but out of a gentle curiosity. That question is meant to draw Elijah deeper into what's going on in his soul.

Then something shocking happens. Elijah goes looking for the Divine and instead experiences three threatening forces: an earthquake, a fire, and a rushing wind. Each is a decidedly unsafe experience for Elijah. But there it was. And then after the threats, a soft sound, a "sound of sheer silence," comes. If an earthquake, fire, or rushing wind threatens us, it also prepares us to receive an even deeper understanding of how we are protected and kept. We can live between the chaos and the danger and find the Divine quietly whispering our names.

SAFETY AND SEASONS

As I mentioned before, I wrote much of this book from a comfortable chair along the Front Range in Boulder, Colorado. In the near view are pines that were here well before I was born and will be here long after I'm gone. The far view reveals rolling hills where a rancher has been herding cattle for the last two days. Mountains appear to be stacked horizontally on top of each other, but a closer inspection would reveal great distance between the peaks.

When you are in the presence of nature, you see your own size made plain. The mountains, the pines, the scrubs, and the sweeping valleys have been a part of this great dance for much longer than we can conceive. They have survived fires and glaciers and the steel-handed thunder of humankind.

Coincidentally, these views would be marred by a raging fire several months later. Now I hear from my friends that even the pine stumps, charred and small, still excrete sap. Apparently it is the way they heal themselves, the way they rescue themselves from the ash.

As I look out across the expanse, a thought occurs to me about this season of self-protection. The sense of safety that made its home in my soul, as I hoarded my energy for the last two years, is not unlike what I feel in the space between seasons. When we are in between stages or seasons of life, our sense of safety changes. In some seasons of life, we feel more comfortable and safer in our life rhythms. Then comes winter and all the hazards that arrive in tow.

In Illinois, our seasons move quickly, so you must be ready to speedily switch out your wardrobe as well as the implements in your garage: mowers move for rakes, and then rakes defer to snow shovels and snow blowers. And so it goes.

But there are the in-between moments of the season, when you realize the weather has not yet finished with one season even though *you* have moved on to the next. It is the day that begins in the lower fifties but ends in the sun-drenched eighties. You learn to dress in layers that can be removed for the first few weeks of fall and the first few weeks of spring.

As you look at where you feel unsafe, vulnerable, and at risk, the seasons can be a helpful guide. God, it appears, is the steward of all seasons. No matter what season of life you resonate with—the life of spring and summer, the decline and rest of autumn, or the deadness of winter—the space between the seasons is the most fertile ground for restlessness. We want to move forward into a new space in life, whether we are bored, disenfranchised, or wounded by the season that is ending. In the close of a season, there is a threat that we may lose our way between this season and the next.

Some seasons are simply more severe teachers when it comes to the curriculum of safety. In winter, new things are always budding all around us but only beneath the surface. They are waiting, young and fragile, but they are not sustainable now.

Winter is, in fact, a time of death. Though the same daylilies and Rose of Sharon bushes will bloom around my house in the spring, they will never bloom the same as they did this year. The year that has been laid to rest.

Through pandemics, health crises, job crises, and mental health journeys, the winter season draws us down deep. If fall is the receding of life, then winter is the time when our soul hibernates and rediscovers itself. Winter is where we go when our souls feel unsafe and weak. We go beneath the surface after the loss of a loved one or after a long and difficult project ends.

The cold, hard winter is the teacher we do not want, but it is the one we desperately need. When we release our life as we know it, as Jesus said, we keep our souls. Winter is the brutal edge of divine recreation, defying our expectations. And the teacher who knows the way of suffering comes alongside us in winter, whispering, "Spring will come. But not yet."

In a winter season, our restless question is whether the cold will be too much. Will what goes to sleep awaken again? Can we truly lean into the safety of resurrection when everything around us screams of execution?

We are most restless in cold and hardened times. Staring out the window at the falling snow in late February, I begin to long for days of walking without a hat and gloves. "This snow has to end," I remark to my wife. "I can't do this for much longer."

And then winter does end. And the winter changes me. If nothing else, it reminds me that even in the risks of the dark cold, I am safe. "That's what you learn in winter: there's a past, a present, and a future," writes Katherine May. "There is a time after the aftermath."

It is often hard to believe in these tremendously difficult seasons, but the Divine quietly invites us to learn: *This is what it means to be safe. To know that every season ends and to stay in this season with that wisdom.*

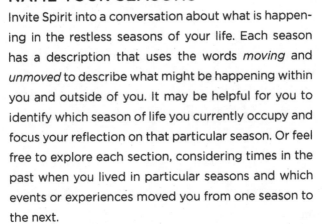

A PRACTICE
NAME YOUR SEASONS

Invite Spirit into a conversation about what is happening in the restless seasons of your life. Each season has a description that uses the words *moving* and *unmoved* to describe what might be happening within you and outside of you. It may be helpful for you to identify which season of life you currently occupy and focus your reflection on that particular season. Or feel free to explore each section, considering times in the past when you lived in particular seasons and which events or experiences moved you from one season to the next.

Explore each of these seasonal reflections with honesty and with an eye toward capturing insights from the Divine. The point is learning how to sit in the restlessness of each season and anticipate the way new life comes, even when we feel that safety is far out of reach.

Spring: Things are moving, but we are unmoved.

What new things are coming to life for you right now?

What risks or vulnerabilities do you notice in these new sprouts of life?

What obstacles keep you mired in winter, unable to embrace these new things?

How is the Divine inviting you to explore your hesitancy around these risks and vulnerabilities?

Summer: Things are moving, and we are moving with them.

How are the new things of spring becoming a full and beautiful part of your life?

What challenges are there in tending to and maintaining that new growth?

How is Spirit inviting you to take courage in both maintenance and celebration of what is alive in you?

What are your fears for the season of decline yet to come?

Fall: Things are ceasing, and yet we continue to move.

What parts of life are beginning to decline, slow down, and even disappear?

How do you feel the Divine inviting you to respond to these movements toward dormancy?

What do you fear in this time of putting things to rest? This may include even good things, like taking some rest yourself.

What is Spirit teaching you about your journey from spring to summer to now?

Winter: Things have ceased, and so have we.

How are you embracing the "chill" of life coming to a standstill?

Now that the frantic activity of the preceding seasons has slowed, what is the Divine inviting you to tend to and heal?

What are your hopes and desires for the spring yet to come? What are your great fears?

CHAPTER 7

CAN WE BE RESCUED?

Deliver us . . .

In an age of screens and levers and switches, helplessness seems like an antiquated idea. I can order whatever I need and have it delivered to my home in twenty-four hours. Everything from transportation to graduate-level information is accessible through the little black rectangle I carry around all the time. "Through the devices in our pockets, we are reminded of our limitless freedom, limitless opportunities, limitless ways to indulge our interests," essayist Heather Havrilesky notes. "And yet, our lives feel more difficult to navigate than ever." With this perceived freedom to save and preserve ourselves, we often distract ourselves from the truth of our own helplessness.

Yet our helplessness persists. Helplessness fastens us to the present moment with a fierce and firm grip. How we came to that helpless moment doesn't matter. Sometimes we have made choices that lead us into the fierce binding of the present tense. Other times we are made helpless by the choices of others, the systems in which we live, or the simple currents of daily life. Perhaps our capacities are reduced or removed by serious illness. Sometimes the choices of our children put us in a place of helplessness, where we feel we cannot act redemptively (or perhaps act at all). The tidal waves of the economy crash over us, sweeping us off our financial footing. Or the career that once gave us life is now gone, and we have no choice but to receive that decision and figure out what to do next.

In the winter of 2021, I learned of two giant changes coming to my and my family's world. The first was that my primary part-time job would be significantly cut. At age forty-three, I would need to rethink how I could financially contribute to our needs.

The second also came without warning and brought a potent feeling of helplessness in its wake. Holley and I realized it was time to go to the eye doctor and get new glasses. My prescription hadn't changed, but my frames were breaking down from wear. She and my daughter both needed exams as well. So one blustery January day, we bundled against the strafing winds and went to the eye doctor.

Holley and our daughter's appointments went swimmingly. Not much had changed; they both got new frames, but their prescriptions stayed the same. I had a different experience. After the optometrist asked me to do the more complex eye scan, she opened a tab on her computer and pointed to an image. "Do you see these discolored places, right here around the outside of your eye?" she asked.

I saw them, but I didn't know what they meant. *Discolored* didn't seem like a hopeful word to apply to one's eyeball, and my stomach flipped a bit. "These are tiny holes or tears in your retina," she said. "These could be a problem."

Twenty years earlier, another eye doctor had pointed out these tears and recommended that we "keep an eye on them" (an ironic turn of phrase if I ever heard one). I had forgotten the holes even existed.

But now things had to be done. The optometrist explained that these holes could fill with fluid and cause the retina to detach. In that event, the solution would be a lengthy surgery with lengthy recovery, most of which would be spent lying face down for multiple hours per day. To avoid that scenario, the doctors needed to act. Like many moments in life, I felt that I had no choice. The watching was over, and action was required.

I had agency in this moment—I had a choice in dealing with my vulnerable condition. Yet that choice had to account for my utter helplessness in rescuing my damaged retinas from further harm.

Next came a waiting room at the retina specialist. Every doctor's office feels the same: The waiting room a caged, anxious space with beaten furniture and daytime programming beaming from a TV. Months-old magazines on tables. Nurses and assistants who say, "Come on *back*" when they call your name. The "back" is a secret place, separated from the common life of the waiting room and devoted to the specific challenges of your own body. My own time in the back began with a routine set of questions and then two drops in each eye. I blinked my way to blurry as the drops did their magic. Soon, everything I saw carried a soft, cloudy aura.

From there, things moved quickly. The retina specialist aimed two or three devices into my eye and determined that I needed treatment to avoid lengthy surgery down the road. He'd use a laser to burn the edges of the retinal tear. That would keep the fluid from flowing into the gaps and prevent retinal detachment.

The treatment included a few more eye drops and then scorching pain from a laser searing my eye. Then all was done.

"No strenuous activity for a week" is what I heard the specialist say. Later, I was informed that "a week" actually meant a month. I wasn't allowed to lift anything over ten pounds for at least a month, and I could do no vigorous exercise or activity that would increase blood flow to my eye. I was to be completely helpless around the house for four weeks.

Late January through early February in Illinois is a cruel time for those who cannot lift ten pounds. The day after my procedure, it snowed nearly nine inches and continued to snow for the next week. Added to that was a firm layer of ice that developed about a week after my procedure. I had to sit immobilized, unable to lift even the dog, who weighed in at a whopping fifteen pounds at the time. And Holley had to shovel the snow.

Without the activities that typically gave me purpose and energy, I came to acknowledge my fading physical self. The situation with my eye was a precursor of things to come, I realized. As this aging body moved through time, any abuse or misuse of my younger years began to bear out in creaking, cracking, and aching.

My sense of helplessness in that season soon became more than situational. No longer could I comfort myself with "this too shall pass" or other snappy truisms. Instead, the helplessness connected deeply with another reality: I was getting older, and there was nothing I could do about it.

WHAT HAPPENS WHEN WE'RE HELPLESS

Aging brings about a different kind of spiritual life. It is the paradox that we have a growing inventory of knowledge and skills but less energy with which to apply them. Aging can feel like a cruel trick, a turning up of the fader knob of wisdom just as the physical and mental life force within us is turned down.

The more wisdom we gain about ourselves, the Divine, and other people, the more we realize how helpless we often are. And in that helplessness, we are restless for rescue. We have no choice but to surrender.

Unable to overcome our own helplessness, we are stuck. Who will rescue us? And what does it even mean to be *rescued?* In your own helpless present-tense moment, how does that word sound?

When we feel helpless, we think—and sometimes do—strange things. We panic, we rationalize, we blame, or we simply lie down and give up. We lean into our lizard brain and eventually choose against fighting or fleeing and pick the third option: we flop. Giving up seems the only possible response.

We cannot control our fading health, the unsteady economy, the consequences of our misguided indulgences, or the actions of our child or our spouse. Our strength to respond dwindles like the last of the bathwater swirling down the drain. We say to ourselves, "I surrender." We wave a white flag because circumstance and challenge have us surrounded.

Many times in scripture, surrender is a move toward maturity and toward hope. Jesus talks of his death, saying, "I lay down my life in order to take it up again. No one takes it from me but I lay it down of my own accord." In the story of Jesus's trial and crucifixion, we see that the adversaries grow stronger and more numerous until conviction and execution seem unavoidable. Jesus gives in to the helpless moment of his trial, where the odds are stacked against him. Yet the story does not end with helplessness or even the hopelessness of an innocent man tried and executed. Instead, it ends with a story of rescue that goes even to the depths of the darkest reality our human minds can imagine. And that rescue is successful.

Where does it seem like the odds are stacked against you? Where have your energies failed to control or solve the circumstances you face? What does surrender look like?

When we act out of an unwise or reactionary place, we often end up stranded. We said *those* words, and now the relationship is fractured. Or we stormed out when we should have remained, creating a sense of abandonment in the person we love. Or in self-medicating after a difficult trial, we find ourselves in a spiral of addiction. Or the church we loved is tarnished and fractured by people who act in ways so unlike the Jesus we claim to follow. In all these scenarios, we cannot go back, but moving forward is filled with uncertainties, anxieties, and possible dangers. John O'Donohue comments, "Frequently, in a journey of the soul, the most precious moments are the mistakes. They have brought you to a place that you would otherwise have avoided."

While we might agree with this idea in theory—that the mistakes we have made often help us grow—it doesn't change the scenarios our mistake created. More than that, the realities our mistakes crafted cannot be resolved without help. Surrender is the only option.

But is surrender the same thing as giving up? The passive posture of "do what you want; I don't care," is that surrender? When does our helplessness become hopelessness?

The difference between unhealthy resignation and healthy surrender is that the latter carries the aroma of hope. The gift of restlessness in these moments is that when we have mistakenly departed from firmer ground and cannot see our way to the future, we come to know our true dependence and need. Embracing our helplessness is the first step toward being rescued.

LITTLE SALVATIONS

The Christian and Jewish scriptures spend a great deal of ink talking about God as a rescuer. Prophets and poets of the people plead with God to turn identity into action and save them.

The word *saved* has so much baggage for many people that it could fill an entire luggage set. In my own recall, the word evokes sweltering campground chapel services with bellowing preachers describing the bellowing flames of hell. All who wanted to avoid eternal torment need to be "saved" by the blood of Jesus, they told us. My early spiritual experiences were molded around keeping the flaming-hot bellows of damnation at bay.

I later recognized that flaming bellows are present in each day's comings and goings. I also learned that the Divine has a heat of its own: purifying, revealing, and maturing flames. God's fire originates from a posture of love, and it gives life to those who aren't content with simply avoiding hell after they die. The flames of torment became the flames of rescue as I reimagined what it meant to be "saved." As Dallas Willard once asked, "What if the flames of heaven are hotter than the flames of hell?"

Salvation is a far larger reality than I once conceived, one that rescues us from all kinds of "little hells" that we face. Salvation is the journey through the little hells that transform us, that shape the way we see the world. When we face helpless moments, the gift of restlessness appears, and we come to see that to be "saved" is not a way out of something but a way *through* daily life.

When we cannot manufacture our way out, we surrender. Rescue is the way we channel our restless energy in helpless moments. In our helplessness, the Divine meets us and gives us the energy to move toward our rescue.

Helplessness reminds us that we need many little salvations along the way. Of course, many of us have a mile marker—a day, a place, a time, or an act—where we begin our rescue story with the Divine. Yet that isn't where the story ends. Our rescue occurs not in one moment but a lifetime of moments. Times of salvation become mile markers we can return to in memory. Day by day, we move into a partnership with God, still rooted in human helplessness, for the rescue of both ourselves and the world.

A PARTNERSHIP

In spiritual direction, I often ask this question: Do you trust God? I don't ask that question so that I can follow up with, "If so, then you should . . ." We were never meant to chase Spirit by coercion. *Should* is a fundamental spiritual contradiction.

Instead, I ask "Do you trust God?" to get to the question I *really* want to ask: "Do you believe God trusts *you*?" We sometimes forget the reciprocal nature of the trust between ourselves and the Divine. But the Divine has already entrusted us with much: with children, jobs, aging parents, spouses, neighbors, and even the precious dynamism of our human bodies. God even entrusted us with carrying on the unfolding redemption of creation. If we believe that God trusts us, it changes the whole equation.

If God trusts us, we learn to live beyond the "worthless worm" idea that many theologies teach, and instead we feel the Divine trust like energy and breath for our every-day life. We do not work *for* God; instead, we work *with* God. That is a different kind of life entirely.

If God trusts us, then we have an entirely different way to experience rescue. We need rescue when we need to exit circumstances and situations we cannot escape on our own. This language is critical because to leave off the phrase *on our own* is to talk about a situation of com-plete *hopelessness*. But if God trusts us, then the "on our own" scenario is not a passive posture but one in which we partner with the Divine in an escape plan—one well beyond what we're capable of alone.

St. Julian of Norwich presents this reciprocal relation-ship as the actual will of God: "that we should seek for and trust him, rejoice and delight in him, while he in turn strengthens and comforts us." In restless seasons, one of the great gifts we can receive is a sense of God's trust in us. Even in our helplessness.

Granted, partnership with the Divine is an educa-tional experience. We are learning about both our helplessness and the way forward in real time, and that path is studded with rocks and crevices that require deft navigation.

We are helpless to return from broken relational trust, for example. Whether we struck the blow or someone else did, trust becomes difficult to rebuild. We need divine rescue to return from trust lying in tatters. So we partner with God, who trusts us deeply, to rebuild trust and restore relationships.

Trust is always a vulnerable enterprise. Barbara Brown Taylor received this rough and ready description of trust from a friend: "Your ability to trust doesn't have anything to do with anyone but you," he said. "You weigh the risks, then you decide. Basically, trust means deciding you can handle it if you get screwed."

Our trust in the Divine and the Divine's trust in us is a matter of openness and vulnerability. Yet that is the story of Jesus: the force of life that embraced vulnerability as a way of rescuing the world. All the "little hells" were put on display via the injustice of Jesus's trial and execution— and then all the hells lost their power. Jesus sacrificed his own life for those whom God deeply trusts. That kind of radical trust allows us to be both helpless and instrumental in the way the Divine rescues us and the world.

We all come into moments that require perseverance, also known as *sticking it out*. Perseverance is the way of rescue, the way forward from our helpless moments. This may make it sound like rescue is all about bucking up and pushing through. When we muscle up, we demand ourselves to be "more faithful" or to "pray harder." Yet it is nothing more than play-acting. While we know our restless spirits must move, we lack the hope to keep up appearances. The carrying on or sticking it out sometimes feels like a weight we cannot bear.

But true perseverance is not a solitary enterprise. In the spiritual experience, rescue is always a partnership with

God. We are not alone. We participate in our own rescue, but we do not rescue ourselves. We can no more rescue ourselves than we can carry a car on our back for three miles. Yet with the help of a tow truck or fifteen very strong friends? Yes, with such help we could carry that car. So the fact that we cannot rescue ourselves does not mean we are left without a role. Our souls were built for participation in every aspect of life with the Divine.

And while I appreciate the emotional force of that phrase *pray harder*, I confess I don't know what that means. Does it mean louder? Longer? With more tears and sweat? Is it to burst capillaries like Jesus in the garden the night before his execution?

"I have found that often when I try to pray through some deep hurt, I find no relief and, at times, end up more depressed, more immersed in the chaos, and more obsessively self-preoccupied than before praying," writes Fr. Ronald Rolheiser. "Often I end up sucking God into my obsession rather than opening my obsession to God."

Questions about prayer often lead to this one: "If God already knows what I want, why am I asking?" In some cases, we cannot even verbalize our request. We are far too bloody and bruised from the battle to be clear about our needs. We pray with groans or tears and lay it all out in plain sight. But prayer is also an act of attending to the presence of God so we can play our part in the restoration and redemption of the world. That world includes our own restless seasons, our own helplessness. To be rescued is to step into a role as provider as well as recipient.

It is to persevere in participation with the Divine, trusting that deeper things are going on than what we can see.

Paul writes to the people at Philippi, "Work out your salvation with fear and trembling." This is a statement about both effort and posture. It is a sacred task to partner in the mending of our lives and the mending of the world. It is a restless space as we lean into that which is already in us and see our character shift into what it might be.

Spiritual transformation fueled by anything less than partnership with the Divine will leave questions of rescue unanswered.

A STEP BEYOND HELPLESSNESS

I could have become hopeless in the winter of my recovery from eye surgery. Honestly, I flirted with hopelessness more than I like to admit. But in my partnership with my retina specialist and the Divine, who shaped this miracle that is my eye, I could participate in the process of rescue. Helplessly so, but still I was a part of the way forward.

In a different particularly difficult season, I went for a run. Skies spread blue above me, with warmth rising slowly as the clock eased toward spring. I had an entire midwestern winter and early spring's worth of rust to knock off my knees, hips, and other assorted joints. Starting slowly, I pulled in all the air I could, stride by stride, one step after another.

During that season, I was walking with family and friends through difficult moments, and I was also facing my own spiritual and emotional transitions as a father and follower of Jesus. What would happen next? Where would we go from here?

Neither of those questions could I answer myself. In some ways, they were the questions beyond the questions; they were the playground of the Divine. Yet at the same time, they are as mundane as acne and taxes. What next? Where to from here?

When you run, you are immediately confronted with your helplessness. You lean into what your body can do, and beyond that, you can do nothing more. You surrender to the elements, the limitations, and the realities. And most importantly, you just keep going. I reminded myself to breath in, breathe out. *Breathe, Casey. Just breathe.*

The helplessness of running soon combined with the helplessness of the situations written on the pages of my imagination, and I began to despair. Hopelessness played at the periphery of my vision, and in that early May heat, I wondered if anything, truly, can be rescued.

We cannot see what we cannot see, and hopelessness tends to blind us further. It impedes our vision. But helplessness has a different effect: it welcomes healing. Like a laser to the eye, helplessness leads us to the divine rescue that dismantles and heals all at the same time.

I rounded the curve, looking down at the trail. When I run, I try to keep my head up, but when heartache and lack of fitness kick in, it is hard to keep my eyes forward.

But in a rare moment of looking up, I saw it. Something blue sliced through the air across the path. The bird was too dark to be a blue jay, too quick and too small as well. The color was almost painful—so sharp, so clean, so unlike the trees and grasses in the background. In few moments in life have I experienced beauty that's so arresting. I slowed my pace. I wondered whether it was a blue finch. The·memory of that flash of blue would stay with me the remainder of that day.

Later, after the run, I would consult Google to find that blue finches are not residents of North America. So either that bird had a passport, or it was something else. When I shared the story with a friend, he asked a few questions and then said definitively, "It was an indigo bunting." Sure enough, he was right.

But that wasn't the point. In nearly twelve years of running forest preserve trails in the Chicago suburbs, I had never seen an indigo bunting. Not one. The moment of helplessness required something more than commonsense solutions. I needed beauty. I needed to see something that reminded me that the God who makes gratuitous colors like the plumage of the indigo bunting was on my side. If that weren't true, hopelessness would be the only real option.

What we need most in these helpless moments is the energy to keep going. Spirit is beckoning us forward, with few answers and even less clarity, to keep stride. Breathe in, breathe out, and keep your eyes open for what may happen in the meantime.

In the restless present tense of that run, located somewhere between helplessness and hopelessness, I took a breath. I kept my eyes open. Sometimes a brilliant flash of indigo is the gift you didn't know you needed.

A PRACTICE
PONDER RESCUE

We turn our attention now to a practice of surrender. Find a spot where you can turn off the noise, distractions, and diversions of your life. You may need to get up a bit earlier, ask for some space from family and friends, or find an out-of-the-way place where you won't be disturbed.

Find a comfortable posture. If you are standing, stand at ease and let your shoulders relax. If sitting, try to keep your back straight without being rigid.

Focus on breathing deeply: full inhales and full exhales. Listen to the ambient sounds around you and use them to quietly settle into the place you've chosen.

Ponder this question: "Spirit, what does rescue look like for me?"

Envision this question with the specifics of your own helpless (or hopeless) situation in mind. Rephrase it in your own words if you need to. Perhaps: "Spirit, what do I need to be rescued from?" or "Spirit, rescue me."

Keep repeating this question or phrase and pay attention to the following:

1. What images or pictures come to mind?

2. Where in your body does this question land?

3. What invitations do you sense from the Divine around this question?

CHAPTER 8

THE PRAYER AND THE QUESTIONS

Holley and I have spent the last few months helping my daughter catch up on good movies. By *good*, I mean the movies we remember from our own childhood and teenage years. On balance, we have finished each film confident we lifted our daughter's cultural knowledge to a new and wonderful height.

While scrolling through our streaming service, we landed for a moment on the movie *The Sixth Sense*.

"What's that about?" my daughter asked.

Explaining an early M. Night Shyamalan film in brief and informative terms seemed doomed to failure. "You know the kid from *Forrest Gump*?" I asked. "Well, he sees dead people. And the main character, a psychologist, has been dead the entire movie and doesn't know it." I spit it all out and waited for her response.

"Huh. That sounds boring," she said. And we moved on.

Summarizing the movie reminded me of the power of the narrative of *The Sixth Sense*. The surprise you feel when you realize something has been happening in the film the entire time and you didn't know it: that fact gives sudden energy to every line, every character, every movement, even every silence. If you've seen the movie, you know the psychologist's wife seems to ignore him completely. When you realize the psychologist has been dead the entire movie, you reframe his wife's cold shoulder. No one would talk to someone who isn't there. Something else was going on the entire time, and that "something else" changes your entire perspective.

For much of our lives, we are aware of some things and not of others. Just like a computer's operating system, something is always running in the background. Simple interactions with our spouse or a friend are what we see, but they are also the result of the story we intuitively use to understand the world that is operating beneath the surface. When we respond in grace to graceless moments, it is often a sign of Spirit working behind the scenes of our will, desires, and intentions. Sometimes these sparks of Spirit happen *despite* us.

In the original language of Jesus's prayer, he prefaces it with the phrase "This then is *how* you should pray." The key word is *how* and not *what*. The lines of Jesus's prayer serve as containers, guidelines, and prompts for those of us longing for a spirituality for restless seasons. Under each line of the Lord's Prayer—running in the background, so to speak—are the restless questions we have asked throughout this book.

The restlessness of belonging leads us to the broad sweep of the Lord's Prayer: a diverse community, a diverse and scattered tribe with one deep and beautiful origin. Throughout the book, I have used the name *the Divine* in tandem with the word *God*, mainly because these are simply our signs to a reality that we cannot name. What if the moment of our belonging comes when we exchange the gendered term *Father* for the term *Source* or *Parent* or *Caretaker*?

Our quest for purpose finds expression in love but not just any love. We find our purpose in the divine dream of love. The rule and reign of the Divine is shot through with the idea of wanting more for the other as they want more for you. "Let your kingdom come," the original text says: allow love to reign fully. This means turning our attention to whatever work, roles, and movements allow that reign to expand exponentially throughout our world.

Contentment is a matter of trust, and that trust is rooted in a daily movement back toward the Divine. The "give us this day" aspect of life is built on a universe that is tilted toward enough, toward abundance, and ultimately toward our flourishing.

Protection and rescue are two sides of the same coin. We hear "lead us not into temptation" and "deliver us from evil," and we know the places and the threats by name. We'd rather not talk about real threats and the perilous potential we pray God will keep us from. Yet there they are, feeding us with the gifts that only restlessness can bring.

A WALK IN THE BREEZE

As I write, the ink has dried on summer, and autumn is descending quietly. Temperatures and leaves and darkness are falling. Yesterday, Winston and I walked in a breeze that served as a tantalizing preview of the gusting days to come. Winston desperately needed a haircut, and his shaggy jowls bore the brunt of the low-lying breeze. Fur and ears pressed back, he looked as if he were walking face-first into an industrial fan.

When we left the house, I left behind multiple things yet undone. I left behind many words that needed to be written, loved, hated, and edited. Questions about God, self, and others lay in wait.

While I walked, one of my jobs was ending, and another job was beginning. My wife was reading on the couch. Safely in her room, my daughter was writing her own story and honing her own craft of words. We talk about her as being "level" or "healthy" because when it comes to anxiety and other mental health challenges, there really isn't a recovery. So as she writes, she pours her life and aches into new characters and stories—stories that burst with life, just like she does.

As Winston and I walked the neighborhood, I let my thoughts turn toward all the restless questions churning within me. How can I best steward my education and experience? Will we have enough to pay the bills? Will my body be strong enough for the tasks of the next twenty years? I have never felt like I "fit" anywhere; do I belong to anything other than my beautiful little family?

The unsettled seasons are ones I tend to embrace quickly, and I can smell the sickly sweet aroma of restlessness. So right now, what keeps me from a fuller embrace?

What does rescue look like right now, and what is the part I am to play?

Then something strange happened. Somewhere between a pit stop for Winston in my neighbor's yard and another on the block just south of our house, the breeze quieted my restless spirit. Illinois has more than enough passing gusts and gales, but this one was different. It felt very specific, very personal, like a gift just for me in that specific moment.

Have you ever experienced something so common, so simple, so *normal* but in an out-of-the-ordinary way? It was nothing more than a simple breeze in the middle of complex thoughts, yet it also felt like a bit of the Divine tending to a restless child. "The wind blows where it chooses, and you hear the sound of it," Jesus says, "but you do not know where it comes from or where it goes. *So* it is with everyone who is born of the Spirit."

I felt the words rise in my mind: "You'll need to stay with Spirit here. You may not know where things are headed, but stay. Above all things, stay."

Winston's claws click-click-clicked on the sidewalk as I breathed deeply. The restless questions settled just as quickly as I stirred them. We were surrounded by normalcy. I watched our neighbor's garage door open and kids emerge as if freed from a long prison sentence. Construction continued around the block just south of us, and school buses and the cars of returning commuters and mail carriers surrounded us. Yet in the normalcy was something sacred. Winston and I were accompanied. Everyone else around us was accompanied as well, whether they knew it or not. They all carried their own restlessness, and they were all eligible for the gifts that restlessness could bring.

The prayer that Jesus taught us to pray—the one that shapes so many liturgies and family events—is a prayer of the restless nomad. It's the prayer of attendants of the sacred normal. It is always humming in the background, if only we would choose to stop and listen.

The questions inherent in the Lord's Prayer help us frame questions around our own belonging and how we attach, detach, and reattach to God, self, and others. The petitions for purpose help us ask, "What do I really love?" The restlessness we feel toward the idea of contentment helps us ask the Divine, "What is enough?" Our hopeful question of whether our small worlds and the greater world will be mended prompts us to live in a posture of forgiveness. When we feel unsafe and when we feel helpless, the prayer gives us restless questions about where safety leads us and how rescue really works.

As we pray the Lord's Prayer, we learn that everything belongs. We learn that even restlessness has a gift if we choose to wait in the wilderness to see it bloom in full. In whatever may come, we can trust that the Divine waits for us and with us in restless places.

Know that the things that feel fractured can be mended, even if we are unable to step out of the torn places immediately.

Know that enough is probably less than we imagine but more than we'd think to ask for.

Know that we have always belonged and that the joy is discovering that truth over and over again.

Know that safety isn't what you thought.

Know that purpose is found in the freedom of the playland, in the freedom of what you truly love.

Know your helplessness is part of the way the Divine rescues you—and the world.

Your restlessness is a gift, so be compassionate toward yourself as you enter any desolate place.

As we neared home, Winston crossed the street, largely out of habit. I strayed into a peaceful place with my own questions, navigating the tension of worry and release. Winston was leading the way because he knew the way.

You know the way as well, don't you? "This is the way," the Divine whispers: the way of restlessness. Walk in it and find the gifts it has for you.

In the land in between, the restless present tense, you are not alone.

A PRACTICE
PRAY THE RESTLESS PRAYER IN YOUR OWN WORDS

Spend time with the Lord's Prayer. Take time to read through various versions of Jesus's prayer in Matthew 6:9–11 in different Bible translations.

Reflect on your own story and challenges as you read. Is there a line in Jesus's teaching on prayer that evokes an image or thought for you? How does that thought connect with the restlessness you feel at this moment in time?

Our relationship with scripture can grow if we create our own version or paraphrase. In the first chapter, I shared one version of Jesus's prayer. Below is my paraphrase of the Lord's Prayer. It came from a time when I was asking some very specific restless questions, and I found comfort in shaping my own longings around Jesus's words.

> Divine One in heaven, holy and separate is your name. Let your divine dream come and your desires come true, here and now, like it is where you are. Give us today the things that we need and forgive us as we live in forgiveness with others. Protect us in our various ways of living and rescue us from the threat of fear and death.

Now write your own paraphrase of this restless prayer. Use each line of the prayer to engage with your own very human, spiritual questions. State each line in your own words, with your own emphasis and desires built right in.

When you're finished, repeat each line out loud. Consider keeping it in a prominent place. Reciting some version of the Lord's Prayer—your own or the version from a favorite translation—could be a daily practice.

Listen for how Spirit is inviting you to attend to this restless present tense. Lean into your irritation and unsettledness for deeper and more significant ways of seeing each of the restless questions that drive your paraphrase of the prayer itself. What are you learning? What comes to mind that didn't initially make itself known as you wrote?

ACKNOWLEDGMENTS

The emergence of a book rises or falls on *time*—minutes, hours, and days—and time is a precious commodity. I cannot thank my wife, Holley, and my daughter, Bailey, enough for the sacrifices they made so that I could type away in the basement for hours on end. Holley, the last twenty-plus years have been miracles of many colors and shapes. I could not love two people more than I love you two, and I am grateful that you receive and love the weirdness of me without much effort at all. You help me remember my Belonging as all the little belongings change. Team Tygrett for the win.

Thanks also to Winston the Westie for providing so many moments that I never thought I'd enjoy with a dog.

Thanks to both Mom and Dad Tygrett and Mom and Dad Benté for always asking how my writing was going and reminding me of who I am when I lost the plot.

To be honest, this book has been around since well before the pandemic shifted all our lives in a new and interesting direction. I had all but put it away in the "digital drawer" never to be seen again, but thanks to Don Gates's feedback on the early writing and steadfast representation, I was able to bring it back to the surface and give it new life.

Thanks to Valerie Weaver-Zercher and the team at Broadleaf Books for believing in this project so deeply and enthusiastically. It has been a true pleasure to partner with you in this work.

Thank you to Jeff Crosby, Jason Feffer, and Robert Ebbens for reading early chapters and giving feedback. Thanks to Mindy Caliguire, Eric Camfield, Karley Hatter, and Rachel Bull at Soul Care for your encouragement and for understanding when I didn't respond to emails in a timely manner while writing.

Thanks to Darrell, Maggie, and John, my friends from the other side of the world. You are good, beautiful, and true. Thanks to James Bryan Smith and the crew at the Apprentice Institute for asking about the book and always encouraging me to write more.

And thank you to Pádraig Ó Tuama, whose poetry wasn't directly quoted in this book but haunted my thinking while I wrote. You have always been kind and graceful to me, and your poetry has been as kind a guide as you.

And to you, restless reader, thank you for at least wondering if there was a gift in the middle of your unsettled, irritated seasons. I hope you found some clarity on what the way forward looks like. Receive the gift in the wilderness, ask the questions, and the Divine will lead you through.

NOTES

INTRODUCTION

"No one yet has found a way": Dallas Willard, "Planning for Transformation," audio.

"Desire is often expressed in restlessness": John O'Donohue, *To Bless the Space between Us: A Book of Blessings* (New York: Doubleday, 2008), 24.

"It seems that we are born with a memory": Joan Chittister, *Called to Question: A Spiritual Memoir* (New York: Sheed & Ward, 2009), 226.

Even Jesus expresses: See Matthew 27:46.

CHAPTER 1

"Everything that happens to us": John O'Donohue, *Anam Cara: A Book of Celtic Wisdom* (New York: Harper Perennial, 1997), 6.

"I know you": See Exodus 3:11–12, paraphrase.

"Dissatisfaction becomes the spiritual director": Chittister, *Called to Question,* 72.

At the beginning: See Matthew 3:13–17.

"You are my": See Luke 3:22.

"Our hearts are restless": John K. Ryan, ed., *The Confessions of St. Augustine* (New York: Image, 1960), 43.

"Jesus was led up": Matthew 4:1 tells us.

In the wilderness: See Matthew 4:1–11.

To be relevant: Henri J. M. Nouwen, *In the Name of Jesus: Reflections on Christian Leadership* (New York: Crossroad, 2015).

CHAPTER 2

"The sacred thing about being human": Kaitlin B. Curtice, *Native: Identity, Belonging, and Rediscovering God* (Grand Rapids, MI: Brazos Press, 2020), 5. Italics original.

Author Charlotte Donlon refers to this: Charlotte Donlon, *The Great Belonging: How Loneliness Leads Us to Each Other* (Minneapolis: Broadleaf Books, 2020).

"If I make": See Psalm 139:8, NIV.

"My spirit will": See John 14:17, paraphrase.

We are ones created very good: See Genesis 1:31, Mark 1:11, and 2 Corinthians 3:17.

"God declared creation very good!": Ronald Rolheiser, *Sacred Fire: A Vision for a Deeper Human and Christian Maturity* (New York: Image, 2014), 215.

Children who don't experience secure attachment: Lindo Bacon, *Radical Belonging: How to Survive and Thrive in an Unjust World (While Transforming It for the Better)* (Dallas: BenBella Books, 2020), 188.

"Letting go is called non-attachment": Pema Chodron, *When Things Fall Apart: Heart Advice for Difficult Times* (Boulder, CO: Shambhala, 1996), 51.

"Detaching from something": Barbara Peacock, *Soul Care in African-American Practice* (Downers Grove, IL: InterVarsity Press, 2020), 78.

"In its bareness, the former bed": Peacock, *Soul Care*, 78.

"If any want to become": See Matthew 16:24.

"Love the Lord your": See Matthew 22:37–39, NIV.

"Metaphors and verbal images bridge the gap": Susan Philips, *The Cultivated Life: From Ceaseless Striving to Receiving Joy* (Downers Grove, IL: InterVarsity Press, 2015), 18.

"Like we do our clothes and shoes": Albert Haase, *Living the Lord's Prayer: The Way of the Disciple* (Downers Grove, IL: InterVarsity Press, 2009), 25.

"Mystics have always recognized": O'Donohue, *Anam Cara*, 202.

"It's easy when we're fed what to think": Kat Armas, *Abuelita Faith: What Women on the Margins Teach Us about Wisdom, Persistence, and Strength* (Grand Rapids, MI: Brazos Press, 2021), 2.

"We are whiplashed between an arrogant overestimation": Parker Palmer, *The Courage to Teach: Exploring the Inner Landscape of a Teacher's Life* (San Francisco: Jossey Bass, 1998), 110.

"That space in your heart that once heard": Leighton Ford, *A Life of Listening: Discerning God's Voice and Discovering Our Own* (Downers Grove, IL: InterVarsity Press, 2019), 96.

"We pay a heavy price": Ronald Rolheiser, *The Restless Heart: Finding Our Spiritual Home in Times of Loneliness* (New York: Image, 2006), 4.

"It was only through looking at loneliness": Kristen Radtke, "The Loneliness Project: My Journey through American Loneliness," *Poets and Writers* (July/August 2021), 27.

CHAPTER 3

In recent studies, 50 percent of Americans: Paul Froese, *On Purpose: How We Create the Meaning of Life* (Oxford: Oxford University Press, 2016), 4.

"Love God, yourself": See Matthew 22:38–39, paraphrase.

"To be human is to be animated": James K. A. Smith, *You Are What You Love: The Spiritual Power of Habit* (Grand Rapids, MI: Brazos Press, 2016), 11.

"When we consider how much": Henri J. M. Nouwen, *Lifesigns: Intimacy, Fecundity, and Ecstasy in Christian Perspective* (New York: Doubleday, 1986), 17.

"Will always have fears": Palmer, *The Courage to Teach*, 57.

James K. A. Smith calls these the "rival liturgies": Smith, *You Are What You Love.*

People like Darrell and Maggie: Find out more about Darrell and Maggie's work here: https://www.orphanscup.com.au/ and https://www.goulburnpost.com.au/story/7725776/view-guests-speaks-of-heart breaking-loss-and-revival/.

CHAPTER 4

"So much of living is in the wanting": Jedediah Jenkins, *Like Streams to the Ocean: Notes on Ego, Love, and the Things That Make Us Who We Are (Essays)* (New York: Convergent, 2021), 84.

The reshaping of stories, images, and memories: For more on this, see Casey Tygrett, *The Practice of Remembering: Uncovering the Place of Memories in Our Spiritual Life* (Downers Grove, IL: InterVarsity Press, 2023).

"You have heard": See Matthew 5:21–43.

"The inward unity that frees us": Richard Foster, *Freedom of Simplicity* (New York: Harper and Row, 1981), 12.

Thomas Keating says silence "is God's first language": Thomas Keating, *Invitation to Love: The Way of Christian Contemplation* (London: Continuum, 2012).

"Recover [your] mind and [your] will": Foster, *Freedom of Simplicity*, 61.

"The ability to originate or refrain from originating something": Dallas Willard, *Renovation of the Heart: Putting On the Character of Christ* (Colorado Springs: NavPress, 2002), 144.

"The opposite of addiction . . . is not sobriety": Judith Grisel, *Never Enough: The Neuroscience and Experience of Addiction* (New York: Doubleday, 2019), 13.

"Drives us on past the pursuit of perfection": Chittister, *Called to Question*, 79.

CHAPTER 5

"Let your word be": See Matthew 5:37.

"Restoration is what God gave his life for": Jon Huckins and Jer Swigart, *Mending the Divides: Creative Love in a Conflicted World* (Downers Grove, IL: InterVarsity Press, 2017), 137.

"If you forgive, your": See Matthew 6:14.

"Christianity has made the crucifixion itself": Richard Rohr with Joseph Martos, *From Wild Man to Wise Man: Reflections on Male Spirituality* (Cincinnati: Franciscan Media, 2005), 84.

"Love your enemies": See Matthew 5:44.

"Search me, O God": Psalm 139:23.

"Lord, how many times": See Matthew 18:21, NIV.

"Seventy times seven": Matthew 18:22, KJV.

"Forgiveness is the answer to the child's dream": Richard J. Foster and James Bryan Smith, ed., *Devotional Classics: Selected Readings for Individuals and Groups* (New York: HarperOne, 2005), 359.

"Essential sacredness of all that is born": J. Philip Newell, *One Foot in Eden: A Celtic View of the Stages of Life* (Mahwah, NJ: Paulist Press, 1999), 3.

"I recognize that there is garbage in me": Thich Nhat Hanh, *Anger: Wisdom for Cooling the Flames* (New York: Riverhead Books, 2001), 31.

CHAPTER 6

Author Katherine May calls these times "wintering": Katherine May, *Wintering: The Power of Rest and Retreat in Difficult Times* (New York: Riverhead Books, 2020).

"If you've confronted some hardness in society": Rohr with Martos, *From Wild Man to Wise Man,* 114.

"So it may be after some great cataclysm": Ford, *A Life of Listening,* 65.

"I am the way": See John 14:6.

"What would life be like": Peacock, *Soul Care,* 136.

"This is the way": The Mandalorian (Disney+, 2020).

"One who moved toward rather than away from": Huckins and Swigart, *Mending the Divides*, 102.

"Uncertainty, risk, and emotional exposure": Brené Brown, *Braving the Wilderness: The Quest for True Belonging and the Courage to Stand Alone* (New York: Random House, 2017), 154.

"Yes, this life has been sweet": Brian McLaren, *Finding Our Way Again: The Return of the Ancient Practices* (Nashville: Thomas Nelson, 2008), 177.

Fr. Richard Rohr is fond of the phrase "everything belongs": Richard Rohr, *Everything Belongs: The Gift of Contemplative Prayer* (New York: Crossroad, 1999).

"Sound of sheer silence": 1 Kings 19:12, NRSV.

When we release our life as we know it: See Matthew 10:39.

That's what you learn in winter: May, *Wintering*, 38.

CHAPTER 7

"Through the devices in our pockets": Heather Havrilesky, *What If This Were Enough?: Essays* (New York: Anchor Books, 2018), xiii.

"I lay down my life": See John 10:17–18, NIV.

"Frequently, in a journey of the soul": O'Donohue, *Anam Cara*, 183.

"What if the flames of heaven": I personally heard Dallas offer this comment in several different public forums and speaking engagements.

"That we should seek for and trust him": St. Julian of Norwich, *Revelations of Divine Love* (New York: Penguin Books, 1966), 73.

"Your ability to trust": Barbara Brown Taylor, *Always a Guest: Speaking of Faith Far from Home* (Louisville, KY: Westminster John Knox Press, 2020), 32.

Yet that is the story of Jesus: See Philippians 2:5–11.

"I have found that often when I try": Rolheiser, *Sacred Fire*, 193.

We pray with groans or tears: See Romans 8:26 and Psalm 42:3.

"Work out your salvation": See Philippians 2:12.

CHAPTER 8

"This then is how": See Matthew 6:9.

"The wind blows where": See John 3:8.